JESSIE WILLCOX SMITH

Journeys
of
Faithfulness

by Sarah Clarkson

Journeys
of
Faithfulness

Stories for the Heart
for Faithful Girls

by Sarah Clarkson

Whole Heart Press
Heart-building books from
Whole Heart Ministries

Journeys of Faithfulness—Stories for the Heart for Faithful Girls
Copyright © 2002 by Sarah Clarkson

Written by Sarah Clarkson
Design by Sage Design and RJS Design
Illustrations by Rob Lamb
Cover art by Jessie Willcox Smith

Printed in the United States of America
First Printing

ISBN: 1-888692-09-X

Published by:
Whole Heart Ministries
Monument, CO
www.wholeheart.org

www.faithfulgirls.com
Where faithful girls share the journey.

I dedicate this book to Mom and Dad, who taught me to journey faithfully.
Because of your great love I have beauty in my heart.

And to my sweet friends, Katrina, Elizabeth, and Lora,
who have each loved and encouraged me,
and walked along with me on my journey.

Preface

God knew that I needed an intimate, best friend who would be like me and understand me, so he gave me Sarah as my first child. Over the years, we have shared a delight in tea times, a love of great books, long walks on mountain trails, adventures traveling and meeting new people, and hours of sharing dreams and ideals. For seventeen years I have watched Sarah grow and walk her own journey with grace and faithfulness.

As a young woman now, Sarah has learned to bring beauty and life to all who come her way, to trust God in the hard and lonely times, and to step out courageously in faith—even when she doesn't know where her own journey will lead. It has been my privilege to be her mother and her friend as she has matured into young womanhood. I know you will be encouraged as I was when you read her insightful and inspiring stories.

Mothers will treasure reading this book with their daughters as they lead them to walk their own journeys faithfully. Young girls will find pictures of real girls who influenced history by learning to exercise bold faith. All women will be encouraged by these stories of young women touched by the love of a great God and used by Him in a great way.

I am so proud to be able to commend this book to you, and pray that God's Spirit will encourage your heart as you read it.

Sally Clarkson

Contents

Introduction

*"And I? I took the road less traveled by,
And that has made all the difference."*
Robert Frost, from *The Road Less Traveled*

Life is a journey, and all throughout history there have been people who were called to walk their journeys on a less traveled road, to walk the road of God. This is a book about journeys—the journeys of four faithful young women who took the less traveled road, and how their lives can be an inspiration to girls like you and me.

Since the very first of my journey, I have wanted my life to count for something great with God. But often it seemed that I couldn't find the encouragement and role models I so needed to become stronger in my journey. It was then that I discovered these four wonderful women. I had always been drawn to the stories of Mary of Bethany, Esther, Mary the mother of Jesus, and Ruth, but often wondered if they were really relevant to me as a young woman today. They were just old Bible stories. I was wrong!

In reading these stories I have found more inspiration, encouragement, and even practical help in my day-to-day walk with God than I could ever have imagined possible. These girls were just the same as me! In Esther's life I saw the same loneliness with which I have struggled, and I learned to trust God. In Mary's life, I saw a willing heart that inspired me to give myself wholly to God. But the most important thing I learned from these women is that I, too, can walk faithfully with God, and expect him to use my life in a great cause. That is the journey of faithfulness.

Each woman in this book allowed God to use her life to change the world, and I look up to these women as models of what I want to become. I may never be a queen, and I certainly won't be the mother of God, but I can be faithful in my own way. I believe that there has never been a better time for all girls to stand up and let their lights shine for God. I want to call other girls to a life of faithfulness.

In our culture today, where darkness is all around us, we have a great opportunity as the young women who will take part in shaping the next generation, to take a stand for Christ, to make our journey on the road less traveled a race to godliness. God is looking for girls like you and me whose hearts are completely his, so that he can walk beside us on our journey, and use us in a great way for him. He wants to use us to change the world!

So come, walk with me through the lives of these four women, whose journeys of faithfulness literally changed the course of history. Let the stories inspire you to faithfulness. Let God speak to you through the scriptures. Record your own journey in the journal pages, so that one day you can share your story of God's faithfulness with other girls like you.

Let us look to these women as role models for us today, and learn from their love and faithfulness, courage and perseverance, so that we may be strengthened and equipped in our own journeys with God. Let's learn together from these women, and let God's word shape our hearts. And maybe, just maybe God will use us to change the world!

Journey I

Mary of Bethany:
A Young Woman of Devotion

When Mary came where Jesus was,
she saw him, and fell at his feet.

Chapter 1
At The Master's Feet

Her name was Mary. "Martha's sister" was what some people called her, but she didn't mind so much. Quiet, yet warm and loving, Mary was of the dreamer's race. Always dreaming and thinking, "With her head up in the clouds" Martha was known to say in an exasperated tone.

One warm spring day, she strolled down to the market in her small village, soaking up the peace of the afternoon. Shrieks of childish laughter surrounded her as bands of little children ran about in the streets, their happy voices mixing with the shouts of vendors and the steady murmur of the market.

Feeling a nudge, she turned to find a small donkey nosing her arm. "Blackie, you beggar!" she said, smiling as she reached for a piece of sugar for the dear little animal.

"Good afternoon, Mary!" a laughing voice called. "You're going to spoil ol' Blackie if you're not careful. What can I get you today?"

"Hello, Anna." Mary smiled at the small, middle-aged woman who was one of her dearest friends. "I need…now just a minute, let me find my list… Let's see…onions, greens, figs, nuts and olives. Do you think you have everything?" She smiled impishly, knowing very well that Anna's heavy wooden cart, filled with piles of fresh, succulent produce, carried everything she needed.

"For sure I do!" With dramatic flair, Anna set to bustling about with exaggerated motions. "It's a heap of food you're wanting, Mary. The makings of a feast. Just what does that sister of yours have planned this time?"

Mary smiled at Anna's knowing question as she selected a fresh bunch of onions. "The Master is coming to supper," she said.

Anna's face softened. "Oh, the Master," she said, her tone reverent. "You'll want the very best I have, then." She helped Mary find the other items on her list and then accepted the coins the younger woman offered in payment. "Tell the Master that old Anna said hello, will you, Mary?" she asked shyly. "I can't wait to see him again."

"Don't you worry Anna, I'll be sure to tell him. You have a wonderful evening!"

The sun was setting in a blaze of shimmering pink clouds as Mary hurried down the shadowy cobblestone street. Her steps became quicker as the gathering darkness, and her excitement of seeing the Master lent speed to her feet.

Jesus would be in her home this very night!

It was dusk as I gathered up my purchases and turned my feet toward home, almost tripping in my haste. I wanted to run all the way home—my Master was coming! It seemed as if every opportunity I got to spend with him, I learned to respect him a little more, know his grace a little better and discover once again just how much I loved him. With all of myself. With all my heart. With my soul.

Every moment I spent with him, the warmth in my soul grew greater. His holiness awed me, his words held such wonderful meaning, his love drew me in a way nothing else ever had. I knew that I belonged to him completely.

I was almost running by the time I rounded the bend of the last street. It was fully night, with the first stars shining brightly, or I might have run into the dark figure that appeared suddenly in front of me.

It was the town's grandmother, a widow, old and poor, who barely managed to make a living by searching the fields for berries, roots, and herbs, and then selling them in the market. She looked fragile and lonely.

I stood still a moment, not knowing what to do. Clearly, the widow needed help. But Martha would be irritated if she had to wait any longer for her groceries, and I desperately wanted to be home in time to greet the Master when he came to our door. Would he be disappointed if I wasn't there?

Suddenly, with lightning force, the truth hit me: the Master would be disappointed if I was at home to greet him. After all, hadn't I heard him say we should comfort the widows? Hadn't I heard him encourage us to love our neighbors? Hadn't he said just the last time he'd come through town, "Whatever you do for the least of the people around you, remember—you do it for me?"

I hurried over to the stumbling old woman, gently laid my hand on her stooped shoulder, and took her basket. "Here, Grandmother," I said kindly. "Let me help you home." For the first time in many days I saw her smile, and the smile told me that I had done just what the Master would have me do. We slowly began the walk home together, with the stars shining happily above.

Bowl in hand, Martha paced the kitchen, frustration and anger becoming more and more evident with every jerky beat of her spoon.

Where was that girl? Could Mary not even be trusted to bring a few paltry items from the market? A grown woman she was, yet at times she acted like a child! Jesus was already here, sitting without his supper in the next room, and once again Martha had been left with all the work.

She set the bowl down and stepped out on the doorstep, crossing her arms as a glowering frown of displeasure settled on her face.

Strong and energetic, Martha was the complete opposite of Mary and didn't understand her at all. Down to earth and of the practical sort, she was also lively and talkative, as well as an impeccable homemaker. She didn't really understand Mary, and it often frustrated and irritated her. This night was no exception.

By the time Mary reached the house five minutes later, breathing hard, Martha was furious.

"Martha please, is he here? I'm sorry I'm late, but—"

"Hush! I don't want any of your excuses," she said through her teeth. "Get inside!" Fairly shoving Mary in the door, Martha closed it hurriedly, as she added, "To answer your question—yes, the Master is here. And has no supper, thanks to you!"

Mary spoke up again, quickly working in a word before Martha could continue.

"I would have been here earlier, Martha, but I ran across an old woman who—"

"I don't want to hear it!" Martha almost shrieked. "You're late! How do you ever expect me to get anything done if you stop to help every beggar on every street corner?"

Mary sighed. "I'm sorry I—"

"You didn't even fill the water jars today," Martha interrupted once again. "Which means I have to go to the well in the dark. You always have your head up in the clouds! Now, no more excuses. Go and get to work chopping those onions!" She whirled around and stormed out of the house, still fuming.

The short walk to the village well, bucket in hand, cooled Martha's hot body, as well as her burning temper. The crisp night air and the stars, shining diamond-bright above, calmed and soothed her as she drew the water she needed and started back home.

Stepping into the warm kitchen a few minutes later, she glanced around, expecting to see Mary busy with some task. Instead, she found an empty kitchen. Yes, the onions were chopped and the other jobs done, but where had Mary gone? Couldn't she ever be counted upon? Hearing the murmur of voices in the next room, Martha glanced through the open door. Jesus sat at the head of the table in the long, narrow room, talking quietly. His disciples listened intently, a few of them nodding their heads in thoughtful agreement, and Mary—

Martha's face hardened. The invisible cloak of peace that had so recently surrounded her dropped unheeded to the floor, replaced with a mantle of fiery anger.

Mary was sitting in rapt attention on the floor at the Master's feet, her dark eyes shining.

All the while Mary had been chopping the onions for Martha's soup, she had fumed in her heart, but suddenly stopped as she strained to hear the conversation in the next room. Something about love, forgiveness, humility… her heart had melted within her.

"How often I fail," she whispered as she finished her task. She wanted so much to follow her Lord, to be like him. Gingerly turning the rusty knob of the old kitchen door, she peered into the main room of the house. Jesus sat at the table, quietly teaching his disciples, and Mary could see the light of understanding in their eyes.

Stealing into the room, she tiptoed around the group of men. As there were no chairs left, she sank to the floor at the Master's feet. There was so much to learn!

The time flew by. Mary sat oblivious to all but the Master and his words, which were like water to her thirsty soul. Her spirit grew calm within her. Happiness flowed through her veins.

Then, suddenly, the flow of Jesus' words ceased. At the same instant, Mary felt the mood change in the room, the calm and peace dispelled as the air grew thick with tension. She turned. *Martha.* She was standing stolidly in the doorway, arms across her chest, her black eyes snapping and her frown menacing.

"Master!" Martha burst out indignantly. "Do you not care that my sister has left me to do all the work alone?"

Mary's cheeks burned with shame. She glanced at Jesus, who was gazing silently at Martha.

"Well," Martha sputtered, "tell her to help me, Master!"

Mary slowly rose to her feet, her head hung low and her cheeks burning with guilt and shame as she moved toward the door. To have to leave the presence of Jesus in such disgrace!

But the Master's voice brought her to an abrupt halt. "Martha, Martha," he began, his voice gentle. "You are worried and bothered about so many things." Without warning, he reached for Mary's hand and squeezed it tightly. She felt his love, knew he didn't condemn her. Peace and joy seemed to flow from his heart to her own. "Mary has chosen the good part," he said, still speaking to Martha. "And it shall not be taken away from her."

Martha's face turned deadly white, and for a few stunned seconds she stood like a statue in the doorway. Then she fled the room, hands over her face.

Mary rose quickly. "I must go to her," she murmured. She knew from his nod and smile that Jesus understood, and she followed her sister, this time, not out of guilt but out of love.

The cool night air breathed about my face as I opened the door and hurried down the steps. I knew where Martha would be, and I knew she would need comfort after the rebuke of the Master.

My heart ached for my sister. I loved her so much, and her responsibilities had been heavy after our parents' death. She had never been able to slow down long enough to simply be with the Master, to enjoy the peace of his presence, and tonight she had suffered a blow to her pride because of it.

I sat down beside her on the stone bench outside the kitchen door and put my arms around her. She didn't look at me, but she relaxed against me, sniffling, instead of stiffening like she sometimes did. Finally she lifted her head and began to talk.

"Oh Mary, I've been so wrong," she began forlornly. "I have worked so hard for the Master—making him meals, preparing our house for him. It's what I do. It's what I'm good at. Martha, the homemaker." She attempted a weak smile, but her eyes filled with tears and I hugged her even tighter.

"I did want to serve him," she said sadly. "But I got so caught up in my own capability, I lost the desire to be with him. I wanted to impress him instead of love him. I put cooking above God! Can you imagine?"

"He knows your heart," I tried to soothe her.

"That's what I'm afraid of," she said. "Mary, do you think he can forgive me? Will I still be able to have the

'good part' that you have with him?"

"Of course you will," I told her. "You know the Master's love goes beyond anything we could ever imagine, Martha."

Sensing that silence would do more for my sister than hundreds of well-meant words, I didn't try to say any more. We sat together until she calmed down, and then we re-entered the house together, both of our hearts at peace, both of us eager now to sit at the Master's feet.

This story is taken from Luke 10:38-42

Reflections

I was irritated, plain and simple, and becoming more and more upset as I moved from one chore to the next. It just wasn't fair! Why did *I* have to do so much work for people when someone *else* had invited them to come to our house? And why was it that every person my parents invited over had young kids that *I* was expected to take care of?

It seemed as if we were always having people over, always serving some guest or another. I was tired of it, and I wanted everyone to know it. As I walked into the kitchen to make a salad, my next chore, I sighed heavily. *This is so unfair,* my sigh was meant to communicate to my mother, who stood at the counter making a batch of soup.

To my annoyance, she continued to cut up the chicken on the counter and stir the pot on the stove, ignoring my exaggerated sigh. I knew Mom probably wasn't sympathetic to my point of view, but I was determined to let her know about it anyway. Finally, after ten minutes, when I felt I was about to pop, I turned to her and burst out, "It's just not fair! I'm so tired of cooking and cleaning and taking care of other people's kids without getting anything in return! Arghh!"

I thought I saw sympathy as well as reproach in Mom's eyes, but I could tell she was about to talk with me in no uncertain terms about my attitude. Then, before she could say anything, the doorbell rang. Our dinner guests had arrived.

Clenching my hands in frustration, I told Mom I'd be right back, then raced down the stairs and into my room for just a few minutes of peace before having to face everyone. "All right, Lord," I muttered through clenched teeth as I flopped on my bed, "It's up to you, because I'm sure not feeling very friendly right now."

Because I knew I should read my Bible, I did, opening to a few favorite verses about serving, trying to talk myself into a good attitude. But it wasn't working. Then I picked up my notebook and flipped through it, finding the story I had written for this chapter about Mary and Martha and quickly reading through it.

Oh my—talk about practicing what you preach! I instantly saw the Martha I had become. In a moment my whole outlook was changed by the sudden realization that I had been bustling around the house with the very same attitude Martha had demonstrated, and almost the same words she'd said, on that night so long ago. Rolling my eyes at my own hypocrisy, I prayed then and there for a Mary heart, chuckling to myself about the gentle way God had found to convict me.

I realized that I had gotten so caught up in my resentment over cleaning and cooking and babysitting that I had lost sight of the whole reason we had people into our home—to reach out to them and show them God's love. I had focused only on my own needs and desires and thought nothing at all about the family coming that night. Because of my selfishness and my choice not to focus on God, I had become completely caught up in my own irritation.

Once I prayed, I started thinking about the family in the next room. I thought about how sincere and sweet they were, I thought about their need for friends, I thought about the encouragement my parents could give them if I would serve by watching the kids. God showed me all the good things that the evening could bring, and my heart was changed. I retreated from my Martha position and once again became Mary, with my heart focused on the Master.

Mary and Martha are both symbols of the choices that each of us make. Martha chose to focus on herself and all the work and irritation the evening would bring. Mary chose to focus on the Master, knowing that listening to his words was even more important than hospitality. Martha wasn't wrong to be hospitable, but when she forgot to look at Jesus and serve him out of the love in her heart, her hospitality lost its edge. She might as well not have gone to any of her trouble.

As you go about your days, what choice will you make? Will you be Martha (as I so often am), bustling about, focusing on self, getting caught up in details instead of love? Or will you be Mary, focusing on God, putting love above details, serving others from the heart? I don't know about you, but I want to be a Mary. I want to sit at the feet of the Master in everything I do, so that he can say to me some day that I found the "good part."

Read: Luke 10:40-42

Reflect:

What do you think Jesus was talking about when he said that Martha was worried and troubled about many things? What things are you troubled about in your life? What do you think the "good part" is? Do you think that you have to make a conscious choice to choose the "good part" at times?

Read: Philippians 4:6-7

Reflect:

What are we never to do, according to these verses? What three things does Paul say should accompany our requests? What will guard our hearts and minds if we do these things? Can you think of a time recently when you have been anxious about something? How did you respond? How could you respond differently, according to this passage?

Read: Matthew 6:25-34

Reflect:

God loves us, and will always allow what is best for us, so we needn't worry about the little things in life. What are some things that you worry needlessly about? It could even be things like your appearance, your hair, etc. How can you have more of a Mary heart, focusing on the truly important things?

Read: 1 Peter 5:7

Reflect:

Why are we to cast all our cares upon God? With what cares do you struggle? How can you cast them on God and trust him in your worries?

Journey 1 *Mary of Bethany*

Journey Journal

Chapter 2
Waiting for Peace

She thought she had wept every tear within her. She had pleaded in her heart for him to come back, sobbed, wept until she was worn and spent. Yet, as she watched the funeral procession winding up the hill through the morning fog, the tears welled up in her eyes again, and she could not hold them back. Kneeling by the cold window, peering in agony out at the gray sky, she clasped her hands, and the river of her grief swept over them.

"Mary, pull yourself together," came Martha's strained whisper. "The mourners will be here any minute. You must get over this; you'll make yourself sick with all this useless crying. It won't bring him back. You must stop!"

Stop! How could she stop? She would never see him again—Lazarus, her dear brother. Never again see the brown eyes that seemed to look straight into her heart. Never again hear his merry laughter. Never again feel his protection or know his guidance. He was gone, gone forever.

Rising, Mary pulled the heavy black shawl of mourning over her head. She had to face the day. Soon dozens of people would crowd into their home to try to comfort them, console them.

If only Jesus would come, she thought, her Master, whom she loved with all her heart. If only he had come when they'd first sent news that Lazarus was sick.

She had to wonder why Jesus had delayed his coming for so long. Why hadn't he started for Bethany right away, when he'd first had word that his dear friend Lazarus was sick? It was only a day's journey to Bethany from the place where he'd received the news, and yet he had lingered on for four more days. Why hadn't he come?

For two days the question had troubled Mary. Then, just this morning, on the razor edge between sleep and wakefulness, a phrase had suddenly come to her: *Be still and know that I am God.* Where had she heard it? From Jesus? In the synagogue?

She wasn't sure. But with the words, she had been able to put her anxious questions to rest. Jesus her Master was good and loving and all-powerful. She knew she could trust him—even if she didn't understand. She would wait, knowing in her heart that God could use even the worst of sorrows for good.

Following Martha out the door, she shivered and drew her cloak more closely about her. The cool, damp air was filled with the cries and sobs of the many mourners come to comfort and to grieve, gathering now in a black mass around the two silent sisters who greeted them.

Someone led Mary back into the house. She sat, dry-eyed once more, not speaking unless spoken to, numb, exhausted. She just wanted it to be over. She wanted to be left alone.

She looked around for her sister and saw her through the window, pacing nervously in the courtyard. Martha's shoulders sagged, and her characteristic energy seemed to have disappeared. Every now and then, Mary observed, Martha lifted a hand to swipe at a sly tear, escaped down her cheek from the reservoir she must be fighting to hold back.

Waiting, Mary thought—as she herself was waiting. But for what?

"They are here!" she heard a sudden shout over the noisy crowd. "They have come! Jesus and the twelve!"

Something in Mary seemed to let go at the words. Something lightened, relaxed. Jesus was here. Whatever happened, it would be all right. He loved her.

Though she longed to see him, she knew that a crowd would already be gathered around him. She would continue to wait. He would come.

She watched through the window as Martha, impatient as always, rushed toward Jesus, clawing her way through the crowd.

"Master! Master!"

Her words rang out as she stopped in front of Jesus, breathless and upset: "O Lord, if only you had been here, my brother would not have died!"

Once again Mary shivered, this time not from the damp air but from the anger in her sister's voice. The accusation hung in the air: *Why didn't you come when we needed you?*

Martha heard the harshness of her tone and was sorry for it, sorry enough to soften her accusation with her next words: "I know, Lord, that even now, whatever you ask will be given you." But she said the words without hope.

Jesus looked at her tenderly, reached out, and placed a reassuring hand on her shoulder. *I love you, daughter,* his eyes seemed to say. *Love me. Trust me. Have faith.*

If only she could!

"Martha," he said. The single word had a sudden, stilling effect on her.

Jesus looked deep into her eyes. "Your brother will rise again."

Her heart sank. She didn't need his platitudes. "Yes Lord," she answered wearily. "I know. In the resurrection."

She believed in the resurrection. She knew what Jesus said was true. But how far away and hopeless the resurrection seemed now! It was hard to wait for a future resurrection when her sorrow was so present.

"Martha," he said again. And again, hearing him speak her name stilled her. He wasn't reproachful…only loving. Completely loving.

"I am the resurrection and the life," he said quietly. "He who believes in me will live, even though he dies; and whoever lives and believes in me will never die. Do you believe this?"

His eyes searched her face, and something in Martha finally broke down. She could not resist his love. "Yes Lord, I do believe. You are the Christ, the Son of God come into the world."

She had never been more sincere. Yes, she had always called Jesus "Master," always believed he was God. But her heart had never been in submission to him. Saying the words now, the last barrier came down in her heart, and peace, the peace that comes of trusting God, flowed in. Faith was born in her soul. Maybe, finally, she thought, she was finding the "good part" that Mary had already found.

She bowed her head. After a moment, she lifted her eyes, smiled, and said, "Come. Mary is waiting."

Watching through the window, Mary had seen the exchange between Martha and Jesus, but not heard their low conversation beyond her sister's first accusing words. Whatever the Master had said, it seemed to have calmed Martha's spirit, and for that Mary was grateful. Now it was time to accept his comfort for herself.

She pushed her way out the door and threaded her way through the throng toward Jesus, pulled by the love in his eyes. She hardly noticed the women following her until Martha stepped forward and stopped them while Mary went on, holding them back at a respectful distance so Mary and Jesus could have a moment alone.

"O Lord," she cried when she reached him, falling at his feet. A sob shook her body. "If only you had been here, my brother would not have died."

The same words Martha had spoken—but not the same. Mary's cry was not an accusation, not an angry question, only a plea for comfort from her greatest Comforter.

And he gave it, without restraint, kneeling, taking her cold hand in his warm one, wiping a tear from her cheek. Broken and crushed before him she kneeled, yet her faith was not shaken. No, she didn't understand why he hadn't come earlier—but she trusted him. Completely. She trusted his love.

Tears came to his eyes as she gazed at him, spilling onto his cheeks. He held her hands for a moment longer, then stood and pulled her to her feet. "Where have they laid him?"

One of the mourners who stood nearby heard Jesus' question. "Here, Lord, we'll show you."

The crowd snaked quietly up the hill to the tomb where Lazarus lay, but hung back as Jesus approached it, giving him space to grieve for his friend. Even Mary and Martha stood at a respectful distance as he placed his hand on the stone and wept.

He weeps for more than my brother, Mary thought with sudden insight. *He weeps for me and for Martha. He weeps for the consequences that sin has wrought on God's children, weeps for all our suffering, all our pain.*

"How Jesus must have loved Lazarus," she heard a small girl, folded in her mother's arms, whisper behind her.

An old woman standing to her right snorted derisively. "Loved him! Ha. You'd think a man who could heal the blind could have come in time to save his friend's life," she muttered. Mary cringed as several onlookers murmured agreement.

A sudden hush came over the mourners as Jesus straightened and looked toward his disciples. "Take away the stone!"

What?

Unbelievable, incredible!

Jesus' words echoed in the silence. Several women at the front of the crowd cleared their throats as if to speak, but refrained. Mary could almost hear their silent words: *Is he mad?*

"Lord." Martha, her voice for once soft and timid, finally spoke. "Lazarus has been dead for four days now. He… It… The stench, Master. It will be awful."

Standing on tiptoes to see, the crowd pressed forward. "Leave it to practical Martha. She'll handle it," someone whispered.

"Martha," came Jesus' voice, "did I not tell you that if you believe, you would see the glory of God?"

It wasn't a question, really; it was a quiet assurance, a gentle rebuke of her unbelief. Martha, white-faced and uncharacteristically silent, turned to Mary and laid her head on her sister's shoulder. For once, the older sought comfort in the younger, and Mary rose to the challenge, tenderly stroking Martha's cheek.

Then, standing tall and confident, Jesus lifted his face toward heaven and prayed loudly: "Father, I thank you that you have heard me. I know that you always hear me, but I say this for the benefit of the people standing here, that they may believe that you sent me."

His eyes swept over the suddenly restless mourners. An air of anticipation and excitement hung over the crowd as four of the disciples, heaving and pushing, rolled the huge stone away from the door of the tomb. They fell back as Jesus stepped forward.

"Lazarus!" he cried. "Lazarus! Come forth!"

The words echoed in Mary's ears, in her heart, pulsing with life, and then light spilled blindingly out of the tomb. Mary's gasp was lost in the collective gasp of the crowd around her. Then there was silence. The light poured out of the tomb, the deathly shadows fled, and—

"Lazarus!" Mary's scream pierced the amazed silence. She raced toward the tomb and threw her arms about the white-swathed figure that stood in the opening. Bursting through the clouds, sunlight washed over them, purging any darkness that was left in the brightness of its joyous light.

A shout rose from the crowd, followed by cries of delight, bewilderment, and amazement.

"He's alive! God be praised!"

"Lazarus! He lives!"

"Glory be to God in heaven!"

Now both sisters clung to their brother, who was, indeed, alive! Turning, Mary threw her arms about Jesus, her silent tears and joyful face speaking her thanks more than words ever could.

Jesus laughed with pure joy. "Take off the grave clothes and let him go!"

A moment later, throwing aside their dark cloaks of mourning—laughing, crying, singing in joy, reveling in the light of life—the crowd carried Lazarus away to be fed and clothed like a king.

Mary, Martha at her side, gazed at the empty tomb in wonder. Once cold and shadowy with death, it now stood drenched in sunlight, lit from within and without with life. Once a symbol of sorrow and death, now it stood as a symbol of Jesus' power over death.

Be still and know that I am God.

His promise, her belief. Mary had waited patiently, and the Master had answered her cry and blessed her beyond anything she might have imagined. Her heart rose in thanksgiving. Never would she doubt, for his faithfulness never failed.

This story is taken from John 11: 1-45

Reflections

Heavy and cold, the darkness hung around me, and I pulled a blanket around my shoulders as I crept quietly out of bed. Tiptoeing to my window, I peeked out and saw a black winter sky with not even a tiny gleam of morning light to signal dawn. Just what I wanted. I had an important task ahead of me, one that required solitude and silence, just suited to the early morning hours. And to be completely honest, the darkness fit my mood.

I had come to a crisis point. Discouragement had been building gradually over weeks, perhaps months, but now it had climaxed in a deep depression that seemed to weigh on me all the time. After all my hard work, my faithfulness, my patience, God still wasn't changing my circumstances. The fact that every other girl I knew was struggling with the same problems discouraged me even more. Did it really matter to God that I waited and was faithful?

With that question in mind, I set to work early in the morning. I was determined to do everything possible to show God that I was trying. If he still didn't bless me, it wouldn't be because I hadn't tried.

I always start my quiet times with a psalm, and that morning my Bible fell open to Psalm 40. The first words I read almost jumped off the page at me: "I waited patiently for the Lord; he turned to me and heard my cry" (v. 1).

I *had* been patient. I *wanted* God to hear my cry. When was he going to do it? Hadn't I already waited long enough? It wasn't fair of God to ask me to wait longer!

Frustrated, I flipped through the pages of my Bible quickly, looking for something else. My eyes fell on Lamentations 3:25-26: "The Lord is good to those whose hope is in him, to the one who seeks him; it is good to *wait quietly* for the salvation of the Lord" (emphasis mine).

There it was again, that irritating little word, *wait*. God wanted me to wait even more? Wait quietly? I don't like to wait at the best of times, and even then, it's usually not quietly! But how could I just keep on waiting? What kind of supernatural strength did these people have that I was lacking?

I suddenly thought of the book we'd been reading together as a family, *Christy*, by Catherine Marshall. *Christy* is the story of a young girl who follows God's call to a backwoods mission in Cutter Gap, Tennessee. After she has worked there for some months, a time of trial comes, and she questions God's will. She has worked so hard; why would God allow so much hardship in her life?

Christy finds her answer in a bit of advice from Miss Alice, the founder of the mission.

Sometimes, Miss Alice says, you can't understand what's happening, but you just have to keep obeying; later on, the light will come.

Suddenly it all came together for me. God asks me to wait, to obey in faith, even when I don't understand the darkness or the reason for it. The discouragement I was feeling was real, but God was asking me to just keep waiting, just keep trusting.

But how long was I going to have to wait?

It was in that question that I saw my answer—or rather, another question that only I could answer: how long was I *willing* to wait? How long would I keep following hard after God, no matter what?

I realized that deep down in my heart, I knew God to be loving and true, worthy of my trust. How long was I willing to wait? Until eternity, if need be.

When I got up from the couch that morning, I don't know that I felt any happier, but I felt sure in my heart of what God wanted to do in me. Looking out the window, I saw that the first pink rays of the sun were streaking the sky, and I felt that dawn had come to my heart, too.

When I'm feeling discouraged now, I often think of Mary of Bethany. She is a good example of someone who had to wait—and keep trusting. Don't you just know she wondered in her heart why Jesus hadn't come? Yet she didn't accuse; instead, she trusted her Master. In her faith, I see the patience that God wants me to have.

So I am learning to wait for the Lord. Yes, it is hard sometimes. But I know at some point he will fully answer me, and I know at some point he will reward me. I can trust him to be faithful. I can wait patiently. Someday I will understand.

Read: Lamentations 3:19-26

Reflect:

Whom does the author say God blesses? What will they receive if they wait? Why do you think the author can overwhelmingly say, "Great is thy faithfulness," even in the midst of trouble? What are some of the "mercies that are new every morning" in your life?

Read: Psalm 27:14

Reflect:

What does the psalmist say we are to do? How can you "be strong" and "take courage" while you wait for God to work in your life?

Read: Isaiah 40:31

Reflect:

What will we gain if we wait for the Lord? To what does Isaiah compare our new strength? Will we become weary?

Read: Psalm 37:23-25

Reflect:

Who establishes a man's steps? What does this say about the dark times in our lives? What do these verses say the Lord does? What does the psalmist's testimony say to you about the goodness of God?

Journey Journal

Chapter 3
The Best of All

I could see it in his eyes, those loving, radiant eyes. It was hidden well beneath the love and sympathy that always shone in his face, and to one who didn't know him as I did, it wouldn't have been apparent at all. But I knew my Master. I knew his face. And that night, it was perfectly plain that Jesus' heart was breaking.

Standing unseen behind the kitchen door, I watched as he gently lifted the little children into his arms, spoke with the disciples, talked with Martha—concerned only with the happiness of those around him. He was so generous, even in the midst of his pain.

A lump rose in my throat, and I felt choked. I quickly exited the room and flew outside.

A cool, soft wind breathed through the street, gently at first, but gathering power quickly as a spring storm appeared on the horizon. A few moments later its shadow fell over my face. The darkness shook me, chilled me, as if somehow it was connected to the sorrow in Jesus' eyes.

And I knew why his eyes held such sadness. It wasn't just a feeling. I knew it as solid fact: he was going to die. Jesus, my Master was going to die! I wished I could pretend it away, but had not Jesus himself told us, over and over, that someday soon he would die, giving his life as a ransom for many?

I understood in some deep part of me that his death had to happen. Plain and simple, if I—if anyone—were ever to be able to live with him in heaven, Jesus had to die. But the thought of it was almost more than I could bear, and my heart trembled.

The wind grew stronger and I hurried back inside. For the rest of the evening I helped busy Martha prepare for the evening meal. I bustled around the kitchen, but my thoughts were in the other room with Jesus. When I carried in the great platters of food, I took the opportunity to study Jesus' face again. His sorrow, even deeper now, cut me to the heart.

I left the room, leaving the men to their supper. With candle in hand, I walked down the narrow hall leading to my bedchamber and stepped inside, closing the door tightly behind me. Once inside, I sat down on my mat, putting my face in my hands.

I wanted so much to comfort Jesus. He was bearing so much pain! But what could I do? How does one comfort the Son of God?

I went where I often go when I need to comfort myself, to the little wooden trunk that stood in the corner of my room. Gently fingering the delicate designs etched on the top, I gingerly undid the lock and opened the lid. My most precious possessions lay inside. I lifted out the delicate shawl on top, every stitch sewn by the loving hands of my dead mother; the small wooden lamb that Lazarus had carved for me; the pearl hair comb, a rare gift from Martha.

At the bottom of the trunk I found my most precious possession, both in monetary and sentimental value. My mother and father had saved for months to present this gift to me at my coming of age: a lovely alabaster vial filled with expensive perfume. I was to keep it until my betrothal, when I would break it at my husband's feet, symbolizing the gift of myself.

I lifted the vial carefully out of the box and fingered it lovingly. When my parents had died of the fever that had taken so many lives in our little town, the gift had become even more precious to me. Sometimes, when I especially missed them, I would open the jar and smell the perfume and remember their love for me.

Now, as I sat fingering the floral designs etched on the vial, I suddenly knew what I must do to comfort Jesus, to express my love and my sorrow. Excitement poured through me. I didn't even stop to consider what Martha would think—or even what Jesus would think—the impulse was so strong in my heart.

Carefully wrapping the costly vial in my shawl, I rose and left the room. Moments later I was in the large main room, where Jesus sat teaching his disciples as they reclined around the table. Sweet Jesus, who never stopped teaching, serving and loving, even now in his fatigue and sorrow. I stood quietly against the wall for a few minutes, then made my way through the shadows and sat down at Jesus' feet.

I waited, listening to the rise and fall of voices, hoping for a quiet moment, wishing the others would show some sign of preparing to leave. But I knew that Jesus was almost never alone. If I was going to give him my gift, I had *to do it now.*

With one swift stroke against the chair where Jesus sat, I broke the vial and poured its contents over his feet. The rich aroma of the perfumed oil filled the room.

In the first shocked seconds of silence, I dared to look up at Jesus. Oh, the thanks and love I read in his eyes! He understood.

I cannot express the joy I felt as I cleansed the dust from his tired feet and dried them gently with my hair, trying to soothe his sorrow and exhaustion. Comforting him. Loving him. I could tell his disciples were stunned, disapproving, even reproachful, but it didn't matter. Jesus understood.

For a moment, the room was still. Then: "How dare you!"

The sudden words shattered the silence. I knew the voice without even looking up: Judas, the one disciple with whom I had never felt any kinship. I cringed as he spoke again.

"What waste! That vial of perfume could have been sold for more than a year's wages and the money given to the poor!"

I looked up at Jesus, afraid that I might behold reproach in his eyes; I hadn't thought of using my gift to feed the poor.

Yes, there was fire in his eyes—but not for me. "Leave her alone!" The Master's words rang out, reverberating around the room, instantly silencing Judas's angry words and the murmurs of the other disciples. "Why do you bother her?" he demanded. "She has done a beautiful thing for me."

How glad I was that Jesus knew what was in my heart!

"You always have the poor with you," Jesus went on, "and whenever you want, you can do them good. But you do not always have me."

Hanging his head, his face flushed with embarrassment, Judas dropped into his chair. I was sorry that I had caused him disgrace, but what could I have done?

Then Jesus reached down and took my hand, and all thoughts fled. "She has done what she could," he told his disciples. "She has anointed my body beforehand for the burial. And truly I say to you, wherever the gospel is preached in the whole world, the story will be told of what this woman did."

I bowed at his feet in humility, his words too much to take in. The story of my small gift would be remembered? Perhaps, but only because it signaled the coming event I had tried to pretend away: Jesus' death, his burial. I knew now that his death would be soon. I had given my gift in time.

Quietly collecting the broken pieces of alabaster, I left the room. Martha stood outside the door, speechless for once, her face as soft as I had ever seen it. Tears glistened in her eyes. She knew I had given my most precious possession to Jesus. She knew it was a gift of love.

My final gift.

Not more than a week later, Jesus' disciple Philip stumbled into Bethany with the news: "They've taken him. He has already been interrogated by Caiaphas and Herod, and he goes before Pontius Pilate next."

So the time had come. Mary had known Philip's news was not a false alarm. Jesus would die.

And Mary would be at his side.

She arrived in Jerusalem, along with Martha and others from the village, just in time to hear him sentenced to death. They followed him to Golgotha as the Roman soldiers forced him to carry his own cross, watched them nail him to it, raise it up and drop it in the ground.

And now once more, Mary sat at Jesus' feet. In all her life she had never experienced such pain; it was as if she herself hung from that cross. She ached when Jesus cried out, suffered the agony of his great thirst, trembled at the blood and sweat that flowed from his brow.

Suddenly her breath caught in her throat. Was it only her imagination, or did she smell the sweet, familiar fragrance of her own precious perfume? Could the oil she had poured over Jesus' feet a week ago have so permeated his skin that its scent rose even now to encourage and comfort him?

"Beloved Master!" she whispered.

Beloved Mary, his eyes said.

At the moment he died, she felt as though part of herself died too. The chief part, the best part. She couldn't move, couldn't think, couldn't do anything but cry. Jesus was gone, and the world had never seemed darker.

They stayed in Jerusalem through the Sabbath, Mary and Martha and their friends, and early on Sunday morning three of them climbed the hill to the tomb where Jesus' body lay to anoint it one last time.

But the body was gone. Gone!

It was Mary, hurrying ahead to be alone in her grief, who first discovered the stone rolled away from the tomb and the tomb itself empty.

"Empty!" Martha cried when her sister came racing back to tell them. Together the three women rushed to the tomb.

It was no longer empty. In a blaze of blinding light stood two men, and Mary knew at once they were not men, but angels; and she hid her face, and the other women with her.

"Do not be afraid," one of them said. "I know you are looking for Jesus, who was crucified. But he is not here, he has risen as he said!"

Risen! And at the word, each woman remembered that Jesus had promised he would rise again, and his voice echoed in their hearts and minds and souls. How could they ever have doubted?

The angel laughed out loud at their excitement.

"Come and see the place where he lay. Then go quickly, and tell his disciples that he has risen from the dead and is going ahead of them into Galilee. There they will see him. Now I have told you, go in the joy of the Lord!"

They leaped up, laughing and crying, dropping the vials they had brought to anoint a dead man who was no longer dead, running toward the city, racing to be the first to tell the joyous news. Tearing the black cloak of mourning from around her, Mary flung it aside and felt the sun on her face and the wind in her hair, and knew the most wonderful sense of freedom she had ever experienced.

Jesus was alive. Her Master had conquered death.

He appeared to me many times in the weeks to come, and to the disciples and others who loved him. He taught us, he loved us, he gave us as much as he could in the days before his return to heaven. I cherished the moments I had with him, each one placed in the treasure chest of my heart to keep for the times I would need their strength to stay faithful to my Master.

Finally the day came when Jesus called us together on the beautiful, rolling green hills outside the city. "Go!" he said. "Go and make disciples of all nations! Tell them about me and my love!" I listened as Jesus stood on the hill, the wind blowing his hair, the sun lighting his face, and I made a silent vow to do all I could to bring others to the love of my Master. New purpose was born in the hearts of many that day.

Suddenly everything became quiet—even the wind calmed and the birds ceased their chatter. Spreading his arms out wide, as if he were trying to embrace us all, Jesus spoke his last words to those who loved him:

"I will be with you always, even to the end of the world!"

The words and his last loving look were for all of us, and for each of us alone.

An instant later, he rose from the ground in a blaze of light and glory and music. Light clung to him, and we could see the forms of angels surrounding him, lifting their hands in worship and praise. I shall never forget the sight.

Feeling a gentle arm around me, I turned to see Martha, eyes shining as she watched Jesus. "Oh, Mary," she whispered, "I have found the good part!"

I simply smiled, and together, finding comfort in each other, we watched Jesus disappear into the clouds.

His body is gone, but his spirit remains. His heart remains. His love continues to keep me strong. And someday….

Someday Jesus will call me home to be with him in heaven, and once again I will sit at his feet. Only this time, it will be for eternity.

This story is taken from John 12:1-8

Reflections

I'm a morning person. Of course, it depends on the day, but for the most part I do my best work in the mornings. If you ask me, God created afternoons for relaxing, taking tea and reading! So as often as I can, I get up early, go for a walk, have my quiet time and do some kind of work within the hours before noon.

At the top of my to-do list for the mornings is my quiet time; I try to make my early morning time with God my first priority.

Sometimes that's not easy. My intentions are good, but good intentions don't get me where I want to go when I let myself get distracted. I pick up a book I've been reading, or start a drawing, or glance at a magazine, and before I know it, I've lost minutes by the dozen and my valuable time is gone. Oh well, I think; I'll just be more disciplined. I'll learn to waste less time.

But as I looked this morning at the story of Mary giving her most valuable possession to Jesus, I realized there's more to it than simply wasting time. When I let distractions get in the way of my quiet time, I'm cheating God of my best.

Mary gave her very best to her Master—the most wonderful, valuable, precious thing she owned. Am I giving the Master my best? What does that mean?

When I spend an hour in the morning leafing through a clothing catalog, leaving only a few minutes for my quiet time, I'm cheating God. I'm giving him my second-best. When I start my prayer time only to be distracted by the radio; when I set aside time to study and get caught up in a new magazine; when I make a commitment to demonstrate God's love in a real way to my friends and then can't even spare ten minutes to talk with them because I've wasted my time doing something else—I'm giving God my second best.

As Christians, the Bible tells us, we are to do "everything unto the Lord." I am convinced that in every part of my life, God is actively involved. When I neglect my friends, or my studies or my work, I neglect God's plan and will.

Mary gave her very best to God—not only her most valuable possession, but also her time as she sat at his feet, her mind as she focused on his words, her heart as she chose to trust him even in the face of her brother's death. Mary loved Jesus so much that she gave *herself* to him.

I want so much to be like Mary. I want God to have the best of every part of me, because he truly is worth the best I can ever give.

Read: Leviticus 23:10

Reflect:

What did God command the people to do? Why do you think he wanted them to give the "first fruits" to him? What are the first fruits in your life?

Read: Psalm 56:12-13

Reflect:

Why is the author so thankful to God? What do you think a "thank offering" is? What thank offerings could you make in your life? How does the psalmist say he will walk before God?

Read: Matthew 6:33

Reflect:

What are we to seek first and above all else in our lives? What do you think this says about giving your best to God? What do you think it means to really and truly seek God's kingdom first?

Read: Colossians 2:6-7

Reflect:

According to these verses, when we receive Christ, what are we to do? What should our attitude be? How do you think this applies to giving your best to him?

Journey 1   *Mary of Bethany*

Journey Journal

Journey II

Esther:

A Young Woman of Obedience

*And who knows whether
you have not attained royalty
for such a time as this?*

Chapter 4
Loneliness

I will go with my head held high, Esther silently vowed, *with the dignity befitting our Jewish heritage.*

Glancing up at Mordecai, the tall, gentle-faced man walking beside her, Esther felt an ache fill her heart at the thought of parting from him, her adoptive father. *But I will not show him how frightened I am, I must be strong,* she told herself, heaving a deep sigh.

But Mordecai must have sensed her need for comfort; he reached for her hand and held it firmly as they continued along the crowded streets. A blur of color and sound met Esther's eyes and ears—market women and men dressed in bright djellabahs and veils and turbans, stray animals, row after row of booths lined with baskets of fruit and honey cakes, jars of oil, tables of rainbow-hued fabric. The shout of the aggressive vendors blended with the barks of stray dogs, and squeals of children, and all the sights and sounds and smells blurred together in Esther's mind—like these last few days of her life had done.

Everything had changed, and so quickly! The king's edict, the hurried packing of all her belongings and now this last journey from the home of her whole life to a new home in the palace—to a new life.

King Xerxes, having divorced the rebellious Queen Vashti, was now lonely for the love and comfort of a wife, and it was for this reason that Esther's life had been turned upside down. It had not been Esther's choice—the king's soldiers had made it clear that if she did not come of her own free will, they would come for her themselves. It was the same in house after house throughout the land, for Xerxes was determined to choose from his own kingdom, Persia, the beautiful young woman who would take Vashti's place.

It was an honor to be among the women to be considered for queen, Esther supposed, but she wasn't sure it was an honor she wanted. What she knew of the pagan king and the idols and evil that filled his palace frightened her. But with the choice out of her hands, she and Mordecai had agreed she must go peacefully.

"My child," he had told her the night the soldiers came, "you are my life, the apple of my eye. When your parents died and I took you in, I had no idea what a blessing God had given me. I almost cannot bear the thought of giving you up to the king. But Esther, Esther—you must remember that God is in all and through all, and in every part of your life. Whatever the reason for this, he is in it. I feel in my heart that he will use you in great ways."

"Oh, Mordecai, do you really believe that? Is it possible that God would use me, such a young girl?"

"My child, God uses anyone whose heart is completely his. And yours is. You are faithful and loving; just keep on walking obediently in the path you find."

In the week since then, Mordecai had spent every possible moment with his adopted daughter, trying to impart in the few days they had left a lifetime of love, memories and wisdom.

"Esther."

Mordecai's voice broke through Esther's thoughts, and brought her back to the hot, noisy street. "Come," he said, and pulled her into the shade of a sycamore tree. The palace loomed near, as did their parting.

Esther looked at him with tears in her eyes. Putting her arms around him and burying her face against his shoulder, she tried to memorize the loving security of his arms, and impress on her heart the memory of his unfailing love.

"Be with her, Lord!" Mordecai whispered, tears filling his eyes as he held for the last time the one who meant more to him than anything else in the world.

Finally she let go. With a shaky smile for the man who had raised her, she adjusted her veil, smoothing out the wrinkles before she took his arm. "All right. I'm ready now."

"Esther."

Again, she turned to listen. "I know I have said it before, but you must remember: do not reveal to anyone at the palace that you are Jewish. There are those who would treat you unkindly if they knew. You must trust me, Esther. Do not reveal your heritage."

She nodded. "I won't. I do trust you, Mordecai. You know I do."

A few more steps, and they had rounded the last bend, the palace stood before them. Esther gasped, and her eyes grew wide with wonder; never had she seen such a building, its walls towering hundreds of feet above them, white and majestic, crested with gold turrets and decorated with costly murals. Even the gates were magnificent, dazzling, inlaid with jewels and gold. Through those gates she could see a black and white marble pathway winding through a garden of lush, exotic flowers.

But her eyes were soon torn away from the garden as she spotted a woman in a vivid pink dress, adorned everywhere with gold and jewels making a straight line for her and Mordecai.

"I love you, Mordecai. I love you! Don't be anxious for me; God will go with me!"

The woman was rapidly bearing down on them, Mordecai hurriedly kissed her cheek. "Don't forget," he whispered, "I will be at the gate every morning and most of every day. If you need me, send word." He leaned his forehead against hers and closed his eyes. "Farewell, beloved child. God go with you."

Then the woman was there. "Thank you for bringing her," she said brusquely, barely acknowledging Mordecai. "All maidens for the king, this way!" And without another word, she whisked Esther through the gate, leaving Mordecai standing silently behind them.

The next few minutes were a blur to Esther as the woman hurried her through a noisy, jostling crowd inside the palace gates: "Hurry up! Keep up with me! Don't dawdle!" Finally she pulled Esther through a huge wooden door and slammed it shut.

Then, silence. Esther shivered with the sudden quiet as she followed the woman down a vast hall. Tap, tap, tap. Their footsteps echoed off the vaulted ceilings and marble walls as they crossed the room, skirting a huge pool of water at its center, as flat and still as ice.

On the far side of the room the woman stopped abruptly, and flung open a smaller door. "These will be your new quarters. Remain here until someone comes for you—either Hegai, the king's chamberlain or me. You may put your belongings in here." Then she was gone, leaving Esther with the cold silence as her only companion.

There is something special about this one, Hegai told himself the first time he set eyes on Esther. *Something indefinable, something that sets her apart from all the others.* He was in a position to know; he had already seen all the others.

As the king's chamberlain, Hegai was custodian of the maidens brought to the palace under the king's edict. His first task was to tell the young women they had a long wait coming—a year-long wait. Twelve months of treatments with perfumes and ointments, baths and oils, overseen by Hegai himself. Only then, at the end of their preparation, would they appear before King Xerxes. Only then would he choose his new bride.

As the days and weeks and months wore on, Hegai's feeling that Esther was out-of-the-ordinary increased more and more. She was beautiful, yes, but so were all of the other maidens in his care. Esther had something more, something that radiated from within. She possessed a quiet spirit unlike any he had encountered in other young women her age, including his own daughter, who had conveniently embarked on a journey days before the king's edict was made known (there were benefits to being the king's chamberlain).

Gentle, obedient, patient, unselfish. Those were the words for Esther. Among the women in Hegai's charge, as he had expected, there were intrigues and petty jealousies. Esther held herself above them— yet not above the other young women themselves. They liked and respected her, as did the palace maids. She was a friend to everyone.

Yet sometimes Hegai detected a sadness in her, though he never heard her complain. Perhaps it was her air of sadness, more than anything, that made his heart go out to her. He didn't know what to make of it, and he wanted to make it go away. He would do all he could to prepare her for the king—and hope the king had sense enough to see how special she was.

So it was that one year to the day after Esther's arrival at the palace, early on the morning of her presentation to King Xerxes, Hegai made his way to her quarters to see if she needed anything more, to offer any last favor or word of advice, to support and encourage her.

She was on her knees at the arched window in the pre-dawn darkness when he found her, praying silently to the gods, he thought. He was struck by her loveliness, illumined by a single lamp but seeming, too, to shine from within. In the twelve months he had been molding Esther's outward beauty, he thought, something—or someone—had also been shaping her character, molding her heart. Watching silently from the shadows, he was filled with such a sense of warmth and wonder that he could not have spoken if he'd tried.

Stealing away, he left her to her prayers.

It was time, he told himself. He had done everything he could for her. Now it was in the hands of the god to whom she prayed.

It's so quiet tonight Lord. The silence is like a weight on me in this vast hall of marble. Cold. Lifeless. These past weeks have been brighter ones; but now, on my last night in this hall, my heart is so heavy and full of dread I haven't slept at all. Hegai will despair if there are dark circles under my eyes in the morning.

The morning! My future will be decided in the morning. What will it be? I tremble to think of it. If the king chooses, I will be his wife and the queen of the land. But if he rejects me, I am doomed to live the rest of my life as part of his harem, little more than a slave. How will I endure?

Oh, God, I am so alone! Sometimes the emptiness I see in the eyes of the people around me, and in my own heart, overwhelms me. Sometimes the darkness seems to drain every last drop of light and joy from my spirit; the only time I see light is during these moonlit talks with you. Why have you brought me here?

Help me, God! I know you must have a plan for me in this place. I trust you, Lord, I do. I know you are faithful. Help me to walk the path of light in darkness. Help my weakness! Give me the strength to keep going, no matter what.

You've taught me that being faithful means taking step after step in the dark. So help me today, as once more I take a step in the darkness, a step that will decide my future. Soften the king's heart toward me Lord, give me favor in his eyes.

The sun is rising now, the blackness of the night fading into a delicate blue. Oh Lord, I can feel the warmth of the sun on my face, and its golden rays are filling the sky with golden and pink light. Help me to be like the sun, spreading light in the darkness of this palace and filling it with joy. May the light of your love fill my heart. May I fulfill your purpose for me in this time and place.

I love you, Lord. Knowing you better, growing close to you, is the one good thing to come of these last months. I've learned to depend on you. I've learned how much I need you. I know as I never knew before that I cannot live without your love and light. You are my hope.

The time has come. I place my life in your hands.

Esther had finished her prayer just in time, for soon, the hall was filled with bustling maids, and impatient servants. The next hours were a rush of preparation. Bathed and oiled, perfumed and pampered, Esther submitted quietly to her maids as they arrayed her in a flowing white dress, carefully braiding her thick black hair and winding it loosely around her head, tucking red flowers in among the braids.

Coming in during the last moments of her preparation, Hegai gasped when he saw Esther. "You look beautiful, Esther," he told her. "Like a queen."

Like a queen. Today she would find out for certain whether or not she looked like a queen, Esther thought.

"Have I done everything you told me, is this the gown you chose?" she queried softly.

"Yes," he answered.

"What shall I take with me to see the king?"

Looking at her with a gentle smile in his eyes, he murmured softly, so softly that even the maids stand-ing nearby could not hear him: "Take nothing but your sweet, gentle spirit and your love for the god to whom you pray, for surely he must be wonderful to be worthy of the worship and love of a soul such as yours."

Esther's eyes filled with tears. She couldn't speak, but the light in her eyes thanked Hegai more than words ever could.

"It is time. The king awaits!"

Esther turned to find the woman who had been her guide that first day at the palace standing in the doorway, dressed once again in a gaudy pink dress. Hegai bowed his head toward Esther and left the room as the woman came in and circled her slowly, running her over with a critical eye. Then she nodded brusquely and hurried Esther out the door.

The walk through the palace seemed like miles to Esther, but finally they were there, standing in the hallway outside the throne room, just one door separating her from the king. Hearing Hegai announce her entrance, Esther whispered a silent prayer, and then the doors slowly opened and the woman in pink said, "Now!"

Slowly, gracefully Esther entered the room, the plush red carpet muffling her footsteps. The murmur of voices in the throne room hushed, and Esther's cheeks warmed as every eye in the room seemed turned toward her as she slowly made her way down the long aisle toward the king.

When she reached the throne, Esther bowed deeply, rising only when the king extended his scepter. Heart hammering, she kept her head bowed, not daring to meet his eyes.

The time had come, and she lifted one more prayer to heaven. *Lord, I place my life in your hands.*

The king's breath caught in wonder.

Of all the beautiful women Hegai had presented to him, only this one didn't need him to make her a queen. She was already a queen.

Light radiated from her, the light of beauty and the light of love. Did everyone else in the room see it, too? Had everyone's heart leapt the way his had the moment she walked through the door?

Mere words would never express the extent of his admiration. Esther would be his wife, the Queen of Persia—a queen in name, as she already was in her heart.

"Look at me, Esther," he said.

It was the gentlest of commands.

This story is taken from Esther 1 & 2

Reflections

I love the story of Esther. The very name thrills me, bringing fairy-tale images to my mind. The story of a normal, young girl becoming queen fascinates me, maybe even more so because I, too, want to be a queen. Esther is an example of what I want to become in my heart. I want to be a queen for God, reflecting spiritual royalty in my words, actions and life.

But as I try to become a queen for God, I have to ask myself, *what made Esther a queen?*

Even before the king chose her as his wife, God chose Esther for purposes of his own. Why? What was it in her heart that caused him to choose her above all others? Was it because her heart was his?

"For the eyes of the LORD move to and fro throughout the earth that He may strongly support those whose heart is completely His," the seer Hanai, an advisor to the righteous king Asa tells us. (2 Chronicles 16:9) How do I know if my heart really is his?

I remember a time in my life when I begged God to use me in some important way. I was ready; I wanted to take the world by storm and do something great.

But day after day my life trudged on, always the same, dull and monotonous. Instead of impacting the world, I found myself dealing with my siblings, who didn't really seem to appreciate my influence. My time was taken up with doing schoolwork, cleaning house, going to lessons—mundane, everyday things. On top of that, we had just moved and I hadn't made any friends. I began to feel very discouraged.

How can I be a queen, I asked God, *when this is my life?*

I decided to read through the book of Esther in my quiet time both to find encouragement and to figure out what it was that Esther had that made her a queen in the eyes of God.

As I re-read Esther's story, I discovered something I'd never noticed before—maybe because I'd always skimmed through the early chapters of the book, when Esther first comes to the palace, to get to the more exciting part of the plot.

This time, focusing on those early chapters, I found that they laid the groundwork for Esther's greatness. It was her time in the palace before she ever met the king that shaped her and made her great.

She must have felt terribly alone during that long year. A devout young Jewish girl living in a nation of pagans, she must have shrunk from the immorality and darkness around her. But every day, she faithfully, obediently did as she was told. She was obedient to Mordecai, never revealing her Jewish heritage; she was obedient to Hegai, taking the advice he gave her; and she was obedient to God, faithfully walking the path he put in front of her.

In doing so, she was growing and changing in many ways, going through a great transformation without even realizing it. Even as she was molded and changed on the outside, so she was molded and changed on the inside. God used the tools of loneliness, darkness and obedience to make her a true queen with a heart to serve him. Through her trials, she was made ready to be a queen.

Esther had a choice in the matter, of course—the choice to open her heart to God. She could have become bitter and angry with her lot; instead, she daily chose to remain soft and responsive. Eventually, the people around her began to take notice. Even the maids saw how much more patient and gentle she was than were the other candidates for queen.

When I finished reading her story that day, I was encouraged and inspired to keep being obedient even in the dark times of my life. I learned that God can use those times as tools to shape me into the kind of woman he wants me to be. Who knows? Perhaps, someday, I too can be a queen for God.

Read: Hebrews 5:8
Reflect:

Who is this verse talking about? How did he learn obedience? What came of his obedience? What is an area in your own life that requires obedience? How can you look to Christ as an example?

Read: Psalm 139:12
Reflect:

What is darkness like to God? What will the night become? How can you apply this in your own life? Do you think that God can turn the darkness you struggle with into light and use it for good if you obey?

Read: Lamentations 3:19-26
Reflect:

What is Jeremiah remembering in the first part of these verses? What is the source of his hope despite all his suffering? How does he describe the Lord's mercy and faithfulness? Who does Jeremiah say the Lord is good to? Are you "waiting quietly" in the Lord, obeying him in what he has put before you?

Read: Hebrews 11:1
Reflect:

How is faith described here? If you are in a time of darkness, what are the things unseen that you are hoping for? Do you have faith that God will ultimately bring you the things you hope for? The verse says that the men of old were commended for this kind of faith. Think of several "men of old" (Abraham, Joseph, Moses) who had faith like that. Did God fulfill their hopes?

Journey Journal

Chapter 5
A Woman of Prayer

Softly, quietly, I pulled back the blanket and crept out of bed, my footsteps muffled by the soft carpet. The nighttime shadows were still heavy in my room, but the faint tinge of pale blue creeping in through the window told me morning was almost here. Pulling on a light dress, I tiptoed to the door, careful to keep it from creaking lest I wake my maids. Moments later I was at the end of the long palace hall, and then, throwing open the door, in the morning air.

A sweet, soft breeze greeted and refreshed me, cooling my face as I walked the short distance to my private garden, where I spend hours every day—a wonderful benefit of living at the palace as queen. In the early mornings, it is the one place I know I will find peace and quiet for my prayer time with God. This morning it was especially beautiful, the colors of the sleepy flowers bright and vibrant and the sunrise streaked with clouds of pink and gold.

I never miss my prayer time. My life as queen is full and busy; with so many people around me, the utter loneliness I felt that first year in the palace has subsided. But I know from experience that when I am confused or hurting, God is the one who will carry me through.

I make a point during my prayer time to ask him for help in every area of my life. Queen for a full year now, *every day I grow a little more confident in my new role. Though the etiquette and rules of palace life still baffle me at times, I am beginning to grow used to them, and even to enjoy the life of privilege and influence I now lead. And my influence is greater than I ever imagined. I desperately want to use my newfound power to bring others to God, but I know I can't do it on my own; I need his help.*

And so I come here every day at the hour of the sun's rising, when the palace is silent and my maids still asleep, to meet with him. I love the pure peace of the soft light and the cool air. Every day, I sit under the lush arbor in one corner of the garden and watch the sun rise, praying all the while—a perfect way to start the day.

I was just enjoying a last few moments of peace when I heard a noise behind me. Turning, I saw Anise, pink-cheeked and cheery, peering from behind a tree.

Anise is my smallest and youngest servant girl—only twelve. She was even smaller when she first came to me—thin in body and small in spirit, cowering before me as if she thought I was going to hit her. Queen Vashti, who had been Anise's mistress before me, must have treated her cruelly to have wounded her spirit so. Or perhaps her time in the pagan temple had made her fearful.

Anise has blossomed this last year, though—in answer to my secret prayers for her, I know. Perhaps one day I will be able to tell her about the one true God, and she will believe and become my sister in faith as well as my friend and my chambermaid....

Anise had wakened that morning at dawn. Pulling a shawl around her shoulders, she smoothed the blankets on her bed and tiptoed into the next room. It was time to wake the queen—if she was not already awake and in her garden, as she usually was at this hour.

How Anise loved Queen Esther! How could she help it, when Queen Esther so clearly loved her? It was the first time Anise remembered anyone ever loving her. Not at home, not in the temple where she had served, not in Queen Vashti's service. She was devoted to Esther, would do anything for her. From walking with a graceful air, to speaking softly and gently to everyone she met, Anise tried to be like the queen in every way.

Esther was entirely unlike the former queen. Vashti was very beautiful, but very proud—and her pride was harsh and angry. It seemed she was always in a bad temper, and she had often slapped or shouted at Anise for small mistakes. Queen Esther was just the opposite: humble, gentle, loving. All the things Anise had always longed for. Secretly, she thought of Esther as the mother she had never known.

So Anise rose that morning, eager to greet another wonderful day, with a heart as glowing and happy as the golden sunshine that was quickly filling the room. When she failed to find Esther in her bed, Anise padded softly down the hall, opened the door and crept out to see if her mistress was in the garden. She usually waited until Esther returned to her chamber, but the Tall Man was coming this morning, and she wanted to make sure the queen didn't miss him.

Peering around the corner, she saw Esther kneeling under the arbor, hands clasped and eyes closed, her face raised toward heaven. Anise tiptoed to a palm tree and thoughtfully studied the queen through the fronds. What god did the queen pray to? If it was for love of her god that Esther was so good and gentle, Anise thought, then she wanted to worship him, too.

When she spied her favorite maid watching her from behind the tree, Esther rose from her kneeling position. "Good morning, Anise," she called. "Come sit with me." Smiling, she beckoned to the young girl to join her on the garden bench.

Anise hurried to obey, her cheeks dimpling. Her big brown eyes gazed up at Esther in a trustful, adoring sort of way that warmed Esther's heart and made her want to take the child in her arms. She felt almost a mother's responsibility to Anise, and every day Anise became dearer and more beloved to her.

"Why did you come looking for me, Anise? I hoped you would have a good sleep this morning."

"Oh, I did sleep well," Anise said shyly. "But I woke at dawn and found you gone, and I wanted to be sure you were all right. And I came looking, too, because today is the Tall Man's day to come. He will be here soon."

"Ah, yes, the Tall Man," Esther said, smiling at Anise's name for her adoptive father. Mordecai came rarely, and early in the morning when he did, for it seemed better that no one know of their connection. His visits were bright spots in Esther's life.

She rose from the bench and started toward the palace. "Come, Anise, let us go prepare for him."

"Queen Esther…"

Esther stopped and looked over her shoulder to where her maid still sat on the garden bench. Anise's eyes met Esther's and then darted away. She clearly had something to say, but seemed shy of saying it.

"What is it, Anise?"

She saw the child swallow.

"I…I saw you," Anise said. "Praying. And I wondered…"

"Yes?" Esther gently prompted.

The child's next words rushed out: "Who—what god—were you praying to, my lady? I want to know so I can worship him too. If it is your god who makes you so loving and gentle, I want to know him. Who is he?"

Esther's heart ached with tenderness for the child. Oh, how she loved Anise! She sent up a quick prayer for the right words to say. She had been waiting so long for this moment! At the same time, fear caught at her heart. Revealing her Jewish heritage, even to a little girl, was risky. If the information got into the wrong hands, the consequences could be great. Still, there was no doubt in Esther's mind that God wanted her to share his love with Anise.

Pulling the girl to her side and kneeling down so she could be right at eye level with her, Esther cupped Anise's face in her hands and began to speak.

"I was praying to the one true God, Anise. There are many idols in our land—but there is only one God."

She paused a moment to let the words sink in. "The idols you see are only statues, Anise. Nothing more. You bow to them, but they have no feeling. You fear them, but they can do absolutely nothing. They don't love you. But my God…my God loves his people. He is merciful and good. Even though he has all the power in the world, he is not a cruel God like the idols so many worship and fear. He is a God of love."

Esther watched Anise closely. She knew the girl had served in a pagan temple before being brought to the palace, and she could only imagine the terrible things Anise had seen there.

Eyes wide, the small girl looked almost fearful, as if she wanted to believe in such a god but could not take that step.

"Anise," Esther said tenderly, rising and grasping the child's hand to pull her up as well, "I worship the one true God. Would you like to worship him with me?"

Anise raised her eyes to Esther, and Esther read the answer to her question in their troubled depths. The girl's fear still held her. Fear of the gods—and fear of what might happen to her if anyone discovered she worshipped this "one true God" in a culture of idol-worshipping people. She was not ready to accept the truth.

Turning away from Esther, her expression sad, Anise walked toward the palace. Esther slowly followed. It was not yet time. But she knew the seed of belief had been planted in the little girl's heart, and Esther would be faithful to water it with her prayers and love. She would just have to be patient.

When they arrived back in the palace rooms, Esther quickly set about putting her quarters to right. Then she ordered a pitcher of fresh juice and a bowl of fruit and sat down to wait for Mordecai.

An hour later, she was still waiting. Restless, she found a seat near the window, her embroidery in her lap, and spent more time gazing across the courtyard toward the palace gates than she spent on her handwork.

No one. Nothing.

By the time a servant arrived with Esther's midday meal, she had decided he wasn't coming. He must have run into a business problem like the one that had kept him away from the palace once before.

Disappointment weighed heavily on her heart; she so looked forward to his visits! Maybe he would come tomorrow…

The afternoon was hot, and very quiet. I had given my maids a few hours off, and they had all left, leaving the rooms still and silent. Anise was the only maid left, she had chosen to stay. We sat companionably together, sipping juice from tall, cool glasses. It seemed as if days had passed since my prayer time that morning, but I suppose that was due to the fact that Mordecai had never come, and time always seems to go slower when you are waiting for someone.

At first I was only a little worried about Mordecai. But when I hadn't received a message from him by mid-afternoon, I started to wonder if it was more than a business problem. My concern for him was in regard to a certain man called Haman. I must speak of Haman, who at the time was second in power in Persia only to my husband, the king. His rise to power was recent, and in my mind, unexplainable. I met him for the first time on the night of the celebration of his new position. As he bowed before the throne, I saw him immediately for what he was: in his eyes, I saw greed and hunger for power; in his posture, false humility; in his words, deceitful flattery. He was a proud, conceited man, and my heart fell instantly at the sight of him.

I do not pretend to know why my husband, the king, promoted this man to a position of such power, or why he commanded that his servants and all those who sat at the palace gates should give obeisance to Haman.

But that was the cause of my fear, for Mordecai refused to bow before Haman. I understood, and agreed, for my people bow to no one except God.

But my heart was filled with fear at times for Mordecai's safety. Mordecai did not fear Haman, and Haman hated him for it. I knew of their disputes. And I knew there was nothing Haman would like better to do than get rid of the man he hated.

So, I was worried that day, lest Mordecai have met Haman and incurred his wrath. But, lifting a quick prayer to heaven, I decided there was nothing else I could do. I looked once more out of my window, but could see no disturbance down by the gate. So, trying to put my mind on something else, I turned to the small girl sitting beside me.

"Anise," I said to my chambermaid, intending to reopen our conversation of that morning. But I got no further than her name before an urgent knocking sounded on my door. Leaping up, Anise ran to answer it and let

in Hathach, who served as my advisor. I jumped up, for his face was white, and the look in his eyes told me something was very wrong.

"Mordecai?" I said fearfully.

"Yes, my lady. He is not hurt, but he is in sackcloth and ashes and sitting at the gate."

"Sackcloth and ashes!" I cried. That could mean only one thing: death. But whose? "Quickly, Hathach—go and find out what is the matter."

He was gone in a second. My heart racing, I ran to the window and looked out again. There—I could see Mordecai now. He had been hidden before by one of the guards.

When Hathach came back, the look in his eyes made me tremble. And nothing could have prepared me for the news I read in the letter he brought from Mordecai. I could barely believe its contents to be true. Sinking to the couch, my hands covering my mouth in horror, I closed my eyes for a moment, trying to pray; it was all that was left to do.

The Jews were to be destroyed. The entire Jewish nation! On a certain day and month, every man, woman, and child was to be killed and their lands and houses plundered—all by proclamation of my husband, the king!

But I knew who the true perpetrator of this outrage was—it was Haman! It was he who had sent out this proclamation, written in every language of Persia. It was he who had ordered this slaughter of the Jews, and I knew that his hatred of my people had begun with Mordecai. He had finally found his revenge.

"May God help us all," I whispered, understanding finally the extent of the evil of this man.

Hathach stepped closer and helped me to stand. "You are Jewish, my lady?" He had guessed my secret, but his eyes held only pity.

"Yes," I said weakly, and then again: "May God help us all."

"My lady…" began Hathach.

"What more, Hathach?" I asked, sensing he feared my response.

He answered hesitantly. "Mordecai says I must urge you to speak for the Jews." He looked away and then back at me. "He wants you to enter the court of the king and plead for the lives of your people."

"Oh, Hathach!" I cried, "I can't. You know what it means to enter the court of the king without being invited! Go quickly, tell Mordecai that every man, woman and child in this province knows that to go into the inner court of the king without invitation is instant death, unless by a miracle the king extends his mercy. I can't do it! I would be killed! Tell Mordecai that thirty days have passed since the king has even called for me. If I am out of favor with him…"

I stopped, closing my eyes against the frightening image, and Hathach hurried out the door. I tried to pray. Hathach was back within minutes, dismay written across his features.

"My lady…"

"Go on, Hathach, tell me, I will not be angry."

He swallowed. "Mordecai says to tell you that you are not to think you will escape simply because you are in the palace. You will be found out, my lady. He says also that if you stay silent and do nothing, God will send help by someone else—but you and your family will be struck from the earth."

Here Hathach stopped, feeling disrespectful, I think, for having to repeat the awful words. He looked at me searchingly.

"There is more?" I said, my voice low.

"Yes."

"Tell me."

The words came slowly: "Mordecai says to tell you that perhaps you have come to a royal position for such a time as this."

For such a time as this. Had I not prayed over and over that God would use me to influence this kingdom? Surely this was my time, orchestrated by God, the time I had prayed so earnestly for. To throw the opportunity away would be refusing my Lord.

A numb resolve filled me, and I knew what I had to do. But before I started anything, I needed to kneel before God. I needed to cry out for the courage, wisdom and strength to do this thing that was asked of me. Turning to Hathach, I gave him my message:

"Tell Mordecai to gather all the Jews in Susa," I said, my voice stronger. "Tell them they must fast and pray for three days. I will also fast and pray, and my maids—any who will join me. At the end of those days, I will go to the king. And if I die, I die."

When Hathach was gone, I knelt in front of the window. During all the excitement my maids had returned, and all of them stood together. But when I knelt, they did not kneel with me, and I heard them leaving. They did not believe.

I looked out over the town where hundreds of Jewish people lived, people whose lives depended on me, and I began to pray. Then I felt a small hand on my shoulder.

"I will pray with you," Anise said quietly. "Your God is true. No one who knows you could doubt that. I want to pray with you now."

And so we knelt together and came before the throne of God. The answer to one of my prayers knelt beside me, and I knew the answer to the challenge facing me would come. My prayers had brought me here—to such a time as this. They would see me through.

This story is taken from Esther 3 & 4

Reflections

With a contented sigh, I put down my devotional book and Bible to begin the rest of my day. I felt very satisfied with my quiet time that morning, a good mix of scripture and reflection, and I was ready to go.

Suddenly, though, I realized I hadn't prayed. With a quick bow of my head, I hurried through a short prayer of praise, thanks and a few requests. With a rushed "amen," I was out the door.

At that point it didn't occur to me to spend more time than those few short minutes, or to take my prayer time more seriously. I had learned a lot in my devotional time, and I was satisfied. It wasn't until later that day, as we listened to a biography on the life of Brother Andrew, a missionary to Eastern Europe when those countries were under communist rule, that I began to wonder if maybe my prayer hadn't been exactly satisfactory to God.

As I listened to Brother Andrew tell of his adventures in faith, I noticed that every single one of them began, was carried out in, and ended in prayer. I began to wonder how important prayer really was to God. Brother Andrew's life is one of the most incredible stories I've ever heard, and his was a life marked by prayer. He prayed about everything—from the people he met and the places he went, down to his everyday needs. Oftentimes, he never told people of his most basic needs; he prayed instead. And every time, God provided, even down to providing a cake for an outreach tea!

As I began to study the lives of other missionaries and then of characters in the Bible, I found that every single person who followed God had been a prayer warrior. The story of Esther, especially, stood out to me as one of the best examples of prayer. Her first reaction when she was confronted with an impossible problem was to pray.

I suppose that part of the reason I hadn't spent much time in prayer was that I wasn't sure my prayers made any difference. But as I looked at all the hero stories in the Bible and throughout history, I saw that the prayers of these men and women of God had truly changed history. The outcome of wars and the outcome of lives often depended on someone's faithful prayer. And when I found this verse, "the prayer of a righteous man accomplishes much," I was convinced that it was time for me to become a prayer warrior.

Recently, my family and I committed to praying for several specific things every day for forty days. At the end of those days, we saw tangible answers to our prayers: a house for our friends, contracts offered on books, our relationships with the Lord growing.

God does care that we pray. Even if it feels as if your prayers are bouncing off the ceiling, there is a living, caring God who is touched that you take the time to talk with him—and when you request, he will act.

I want to be like Esther, a woman whose very life and decisions were surrounded by prayer. I truly believe that I can change lives—just with my prayers.

Read: 1 Timothy 2:1-2

Reflect:

Why does Paul ask Timothy to pray? Do you believe that your prayers could affect the "king", (i.e., president) of your country? What are some of the life attributes Paul says come from prayer? Can you see these qualities in your own life?

Read: James 5:16

Reflect:

What does James say the prayer of a righteous man is? Do you believe that your prayers are effective? Can you think of an example when the prayers of a righteous man have been powerful and effective?

Read: Philippians 4:6

Reflect:

What are we to do when we feel anxious? With what are we to accompany our prayers? What will happen if we commit all this to God? How do you think God's peace can "guard" your heart?

Read: Ephesians 6:18

Reflect:

Who are we to "pray in"? Why do you think this is important? According to this verse, what are we to keep in mind, and always do? How important do you believe prayer is?

Journey Journal

Chapter 6
Life-Giving Courage

I was ready — as ready as one could be, that is, knowing death is just around the corner. I looked around the courtyard at the lush flowers and beautiful statues and thought with a chill that I might never see any of this again.

My three days of prayer and fasting were finished, and now a dreaded task lay before me. Strangely, along with my anxiety I felt a vague sense of excitement, as if a miracle might be waiting to happen.

I was certainly praying for one. Without a miracle, I would surely die. I felt as if I were doing the most foolish thing in the world, and if Mordecai and God had not so strongly convinced me in my heart that I was called to it, I surely would not be on my way to the king's throne room today.

I had always been a quiet girl, less adventurous than many of my peers; even that first year in the palace, I had stood somewhat apart from the other women. I had won the position of queen not because of my sparkling personality but by the grace of God. During my three days of prayer I had rather boldly reminded God of this, and asked him why he had not chosen someone more suitable than I for this confrontation with the king. Why would he choose me?

I had felt God's answer in my heart: "I know how gentle you are," he seemed to say, "and that is why I have chosen you." I realized at that moment that I was to use the gentle things in my nature to reach the heart of the king.

Over the three days of my prayer and fasting, I prayed diligently that God would show me what to do and give me the courage to follow his leading. By the third day I had my answer, when God brought to mind the reason Vashti was no longer the Queen of Persia. Asked to come to the throne room to show her beauty for the king and his guests, Vashti had refused, and so dishonored her husband.

I felt very strongly now that I was to bring honor to my husband—to be a life-giver to him. I was to do the opposite of what Vashti had done. So I prepared myself in every way I could think of to honor and bless my husband, the king. I dressed in my most beautiful robes and wore the pendant he had given me on the day of my coronation. My hair hung loosely, the way he liked it best, and the small gold crown that proclaimed me queen was wreathed with flowers. I knew how much the king loved beauty, and I would bring as much of it to him as I could.

I also knew how much my husband loved celebrations, and if I lived past my visit to his inner chamber, I hoped he would share a feast with me—made of all his favorite foods. I had already prepared the banquet. I would do all I could to win my husband's heart before I pled my cause.

I turned to the dark-eyed girl who stood with me in the courtyard, where we had come for our final prayers. "I must go on alone now, Anise," I told her. I had forbidden any of my other maids to come with me to the king's chamber; I didn't want to risk any of their lives on top of risking my own, but Anise had insisted.

Anise nodded solemnly, her dark eyes big and loving. "May God go with you, my lady. I will pray for you."

"Thank you, Anise." It was my prayer, too. I needed God to go with me.

Minutes later I was outside the door of the king's chamber. Taking a deep breath, I signaled for the servant to open it. His hands trembled as he opened the heavy doors for what I'm sure he thought a very foolish queen. Finally, the doors were fully open and I saw the king at the other end of the room. There was no turning back now.

The room swarmed with attendants and courtiers, and I wondered at first if the king would even see me. I needn't have worried. As I stepped across the threshold, the room instantly hushed, and I now felt myself worrying that I was much too obvious.

I could feel everyone's eyes on me as I slowly made my way to the throne, stopping to curtsy every so often as was the custom. When I reached the foot of the throne, I bowed deeply at my husband's feet. This was the deciding moment. When I looked up I would find either life or death.

In utter astonishment the king watched Esther walk down the long carpet leading to his throne. How dare she enter his inner chamber without an invitation! His face flushed and his back stiffened. She was just another Vashti, brazen and bold, dishonoring both him and his kingdom. Would he ever find a woman to honor him?

But Esther's beautiful face was flushed and sweet, and when she bowed low to the ground before him, Xerxes' anger receded and his heart softened. She had taken painstaking care with her dress and appearance, and her posture was all humility. Surely she knew it was death to appear before him this way. Nothing but a matter of life and death could have brought her to this, he told himself.

Then she looked up at him, her gentle eyes pleading for mercy. She had placed her fate in his hands. Whatever it was that troubled her was worth the risk of his wrath.

With a sudden rush of warmth, Xerxes saw how Esther honored him with her trust and with her beauty, love and humility. She was still the same exquisite woman she had been when he first saw her and wanted her for his queen.

I have missed her, he thought with surprise. He had been so busy with affairs of state and with Haman's training that he hadn't thought to call her for many weeks now. But here she was, and he found that he was genuinely glad.

He extended the life-giving symbol of the scepter and watched as relief flooded her lovely face. So she had feared her reception in his chamber, and yet had come.

"What is it, my queen?" he asked quietly as she kissed his hand. "What is it you want to ask of me? Whatever it is, you can have it, even if it is up to half my kingdom!"

Esther bowed her head. "If it please you, let the king, together with Haman, come to a special banquet I have prepared for you."

A banquet! The request was a surprise to Xerxes, indeed. Had she really risked so much to ask him to a banquet? There was something much more important hanging in the balance. He did love a good mystery, and a good meal, too. A banquet with his queen would be just the thing.

"Bring Haman quickly so we can go!" he called. He was anxious both to enjoy the pleasures of the feast and to uncover what it was that had driven Esther to such a dangerous act.

Breathing a sigh of relief, my heart full of praise to God, I bowed before the king. Truly a miracle had taken place. I knew my husband's rash, quick temper. It was only God's intervention that kept me from his wrath.

I hurried away to make sure everything was perfect. The tables were laden with the most delectable foods I'd been able to find, the garden was cool and lovely and a sweet melody floated through the air as my servants played on their harps. I glanced over at Anise. She smiled and made clasped her hands together as if in prayer. She had laughed aloud with joy when she saw me come in. She had been terribly afraid she would never see me again.

When the king arrived, I did everything I could to make him feel comfortable and honored, bringing him the first of the food and the best wine, serving him personally instead of having a servant do it.

Haman was there too, and though I could barely stand the sight of him, I knew it was necessary for him to be there. He fairly dripped delight at having been invited to a personal banquet with their majesties, the king and queen.

Despite Haman's presence, I could see that the banquet was a success in the best sense of the word. At the end of our feast, when the king again asked me what it was I wished from him, the answer was on the tip of my tongue. But something stopped me. Something told me I needed more time. I felt that if I confronted the king right now, it would go terribly wrong. So I said the first thing I could think of:

"If I have found favor with you, my king, please grant my request that you come again, with Haman, to another banquet." At my husband's look of surprise—and perhaps impatience—I added, "I will give you then my request."

I held my breath, releasing it only after Xerxes agreed. Tomorrow they would come again, and I would serve them.

I was exhausted by the time they left—exhausted and worried. What should I do the next day? What was I supposed to say?

Unbeknownst to me, God had a plan all his own. That night, he kept the king from sleep, and then moved him to command that the chronicles of the kingdom be read to him.

I must tell you that only a few months before, Mordecai had overheard the plot of two men to murder my husband, and by telling me what he had heard, I was able to warn the king, and his life was saved.

Was it only a coincidence that the servant reading the chronicles should happen to read about this incident that very night? Only happenstance that the king should ask what had been done to reward Mordecai *for his service? Only a coincidence that Haman should come into the king's chamber at that very moment to request permission to hang Mordecai from the gallows he had built for his enemy?*

I don't think so. I don't believe in happenstance; I believe in a God who has plans for his people and sees that those plans are carried out.

When the king asked Haman that night what should be done to honor a man in whom he took delight, Haman assumed that he was the man in question and gave an extravagant suggestion. When the king commanded him to carry out his plan for Mordecai instead of for himself, he had no choice but to obey.

How humiliated Haman must have felt, having to lead his enemy—riding the king's horse, dressed in the king's robe, wearing the king's crown—through the streets of the city. Having to proclaim of the man he hated most in the world, "This is the man whom the king delights to honor!"

Thus the stage was set for my banquet the following evening: Mordecai, a Jew, honored by the king; Haman, his enemy, humiliated.

The stage was set for a miracle.

When the trumpets sounded announcing King Xerxes' arrival, Esther felt a million butterflies beating in her stomach. Tonight she would throw herself on the mercy of her husband, the king. Tonight she would beg for the lives of her people.

She bowed low before him when he entered her chambers, and rising, brought him a cup of her choicest wine. "Where is Haman?" she asked.

"Here, my lord, my lady!"

Esther cringed at the horrible, whiny voice behind her as Haman hurried in.

"Good!" cried the king. "Esther, what a beautiful feast you've prepared for us yet again." He picked up his knife and fork. "Shall we?"

They ate in silence as the musicians played and the dancers entertained, Esther growing increasingly nervous. *Lord,* she prayed, *I am in your hands. Deliver me, and deliver your people.*

Finally, with a satisfied sigh, the king laid aside his plate and turned to Esther. It was time. "I ask you again, my queen, what is your request? What shall I give you? Whatever it is, up to half of my kingdom, it is yours."

Closing her eyes for a split-second prayer, Esther rose from her chair and knelt at the feet of the king. "If I have found favor with you, oh king, and if it would please you, your majesty—please, I beg of you—grant me my life; this is my petition! And spare my people; this is my request!"

Her words hung in the air as the king stared at her, uncomprehending. But when Haman, with a look of horror at Esther, glanced at the king and then quickly away, Esther saw that Xerxes understood. And he was angry.

Seizing the moment, Esther took her chance to finish her plea. "Oh, my husband, my king—I and my people have been sold to be killed and destroyed!"

The tears that followed held all the pent-up emotions of the last two days as her grief for her people expressed itself. "If we had merely been sold as slaves," she managed to choke out, "I would have kept quiet, for no such distress would justify disturbing the king. But to kill us, my lord!" She closed her eyes and tried to control her tears.

"Who is the man who would do this?" the king exploded. His words were for Esther, but his eyes were fixed on Haman.

"He sits at the table with us, my king," said Esther, her voice vibrating with righteous anger. "It is this vile Haman—he is the enemy!"

Even before Queen Esther's accusation, Xerxes had known. From the moment of Esther's initial request, guilt and fear had been written across the man's face. How had he ever trusted such a despicable man? A man who had ordered the death of his beautiful, gentle queen—because he didn't like her heritage? A man who would seek to destroy an entire people who had done nothing wrong and who added immeasurably to the life of his kingdom? Had not a Jew, only weeks ago, found out a plot against him and saved his life? Had not this Jew been honored in the streets only today?

It was as if Xerxes' eyes were suddenly opened. He saw Haman's many lies and evasions. He saw his arrogance and pride. He saw his wickedness. Unable to control his wrath, the king stalked out into the garden, leaving Haman alone and trembling with Esther.

He had already sent out the proclamation to kill the Jews. He could not take it back. What should he do? What *could* he do? And what would he do with Haman?

"I beg of you, Esther!"

Xerxes whirled around at the urgent words coming from the banquet room. Through the open door he saw Haman standing over Esther, as if about to fall on her.

Like a lion protecting his mate, the king roared and lunged through the door, grabbing Haman and throwing him to the floor. "You despicable man! Will you force yourself on the queen even while she is in my house, and I am with her?" At his words, the servants covered the face of Haman, making it known to all that he was a man condemned.

"Your majesty," one of his chamberlains said in a low voice, "you might be interested to know that Haman has had a gallows built at his home, seventy-five feet high."

"A gallows!" The king was shocked. "And why did he have a gallows built?"

"To hang the man who saved your life: Mordecai, the Jew."

Xerxes face turned purple with rage. "Hang Haman on it!"

And it was done.

When I look back, the events that followed Haman's death are a blur to me now. Within hours, his estate was given to me. I brought Mordecai before my husband, the king, and told him the story of our relationship, and Xerxes appointed my beloved adoptive father to Haman's place that very day!

Days later a proclamation went out declaring that not only could the Jews defend themselves on the dreaded day, they could attack anyone who tried to hurt them. The whole nation changed its attitude toward the Jews, and we found that we had, after all, many friends. Truly it was a miracle.

And I was a part of it! The knowledge that God used me so greatly, and for such an important cause, thrills me to no end. I have learned that he chooses his servants not for their ability to work for him, but for their willingness to let him work through them—through both their weaknesses and their strengths. Think of it—he used me, quiet and shy as I am, to save a nation!

It is quiet now, quiet for what seems the first time in weeks. The air is cool and the garden lovely, and my days have returned to their usual gentle routine. I could never have imagined so incredible an ending to this story. God has far exceeded anything I ever imagined. I am so grateful to him, and so happy, so at peace.

I can look forward to many years of peace now, to a time of prosperity and comfort as queen of my land. I hope I am a queen not only in the eyes of the world now, but also in the eyes of my God. That's what really counts.

This story is taken from Esther 5 - 10

Reflections

With a sigh, I put down my book and reached over to turn out the light. It was late, and the house was completely silent and still. My thoughts were in a whirl, and though I felt cozy and warm in my bed, I felt anxious just thinking about the next day. There was so much to be done: driving a long way to lessons, taking the kids out, doing schoolwork and so much more.

It seemed that I had only fallen asleep a few moments before when my mom shook me awake the next morning. It was still very dark, the first bluish light of dawn just beginning to come through the window. "Sarah, come upstairs, I have a surprise for you," she whispered.

Crawling sleepily out of bed, I stretched, pushed my hair back and dragged up the stairs. I found Mom in the living room, where a beautiful sight greeted my eyes. A fire was crackling in the fireplace, casting flickering shadows across the room. On the coffee table sat a lighted candle and a tray, covered with a pretty cloth, on which sat a slice of fresh, homemade toast with jam and a cup of hot tea. My favorite Celtic music played in the background.

"I wanted to get you up early to show you that I love you and to talk to you for a little while before the day starts," Mom said quietly from the couch.

The tea was perfect and the toast practically melted in my mouth. It's amazing how good food tastes when someone else makes it for you! For the next hour my mom and I talked about all the things that were happening in my life—the beautiful things and the things that troubled me, and all the other tidbits that mothers and daughters can share.

When the sunlight began to pour steadily through the window and we heard the first pit-a-pat steps of my siblings on the stairs, my whole outlook on life, not to mention the day, had brightened. My mother's life-giving love had completely changed how I felt. I'll never forget that morning.

Life-giving is bringing warmth, love, pleasure, beauty, into someone else's life. When a friend sends you a sweet letter because she knows you're discouraged, she is being a life-giver. When you give a special gift to someone, knowing that it will bring beauty into their heart, you are being a life-giver.

Christ, through his death on the cross, was the ultimate life-giver. We can be like him, extending love and life to those he places in our paths. We can be like Esther, who offers one of best examples of life-giving action in the Bible. Faced with the task of convincing the king to spare her people, she realized that if she was to expect mercy from him, she had to win him to her side—and she had to do it through life-giving.

So she gave him beauty, adorning herself as richly as she could. She gave him honor, showing him reverence through her respectful words. She brought him pleasure in the sumptuous feast she laid before him. In short, she brought life and beauty into every part of his life, and in so doing won him to her side.

You, too, with your gifts of love and tenderness, can win people to your side, influence those around you, soften a hardened heart. You can change someone's whole outlook on life with just a few loving words and cup of tea, the way my mom did.

Life-giving is a much more effective way to win an argument than anger. I can tell you from experience, for example, that siblings are much more likely to agree with you when you bring them a cup of tea or a special treat.

When you see someone in need of love or find a relationship especially difficult, ask God to make you a life-giver—and then watch as he works through you. Like Esther, you just might witness a miracle.

Read: Proverbs 15:1

Reflect:

This is a verse that every mother makes her children memorize, and I'm sure you've heard it a thousand times. How does it apply to life-giving? What word is used to describe the answer that turns away anger? What are some other words that could be substituted there? (i.e., loving, humble, etc.) Can you apply these in your own life?

Read: Philippians 4:5

Reflect:

What kind of spirit are we to show to everyone? Why do you think Paul chose the word "gentle" to describe the spirit we are to have? When you think of a gentle spirit, what words come to your mind? Why do you think a gentle spirit is so important for a Christian? How can you show a gentle spirit to someone today?

Read: Matthew 5:13-16

Reflect:

I always love to read this passage because it reminds me how I want others to feel when they're around me. I want to give light to others, bring them pleasure, and show them the Father. How are you to let your light shine? Why are you to let it shine? Do you think your actions could show someone the Father? List several ways you can let your light shine before your family, and then try to carry them out.

Read: John 1:4

Reflect:

Of whom is this verse speaking? What kind of life was found in Christ? What was that life to mankind? How can you reflect the life of Christ and bring his life to others? Look through the gospels for several accounts of Jesus dealing with people in loving ways. What can you learn from his example?

Journey Journal

Journey III

Mary, the Mother of Jesus:
A Young Woman
of Willingness

I am the Lord's bondservant.

Chapter 7
Handmaiden of the Lord

He is so perfect, my new baby Jesus with his tiny face and warm brown eyes and pink fingers that wrap so sweetly around mine. I am blessed above all women to have this baby boy, and even the stars shining in through the ragged hole in the roof seem to share in my joy.

It is dark now, and in our cozy stable all is silent. The last hours have been a bustle of noise and pain, but my little one is finally here, and he has brought peace with him. The stable is warm, and I can smell the hay and animal bodies. A candle flickers gently, sending shadows dancing through the room.

The fulfillment of all God told me would happen has finally come, and I hold him in my arms. It's astonishing to remember that this baby I hold is the Son of God, the same person who was with the Father when the world was made. I am so awed at the greatness of God's plan.

I'm so tired. It feels heavenly to lean back against the straw and pull the blanket closer around us. It was a long physical journey to this stable in Bethlehem, and an even longer spiritual journey to the peace I now have in my heart. But I have finally come to a place of rest and utter happiness because of the perfect baby in my arms. To finally be able to relax at least a little bit is such a relief, especially since I know that God is watching us from above and Joseph is guarding us here below.

Even now he is at the stable door—sweet Joseph. He is so faithful, so good; surely God blessed me when he brought me Joseph. Of course, God has been good in everything, faithful and loving, even though I sometimes have a hard time remembering that. He has guided me every step of the way along this new path on which he set my feet. It has been difficult, and I have lost much from following God. But in the end, his love has far outweighed anything I had to give up.

It has been a journey of faith and miracles, but also one of more pain than I could ever have imagined. But God is good, and now, as I fall asleep so easily, all the different memories of my journey are coming back to me. Perhaps I will think of them in my sleep. Maybe I will dream of faith, angels, holy babies, and remember through it all the night that changed my life forever…

She was on her way home from an errand for her mother, enjoying the peace of the afternoon, when it happened. She had taken the long way home, which took her past one of her favorite places, a private spot where she often came when she needed to think. And there was much to think about. Mostly Joseph—sweet, loving, wonderful Joseph, whom she was going to marry. How good God had been to bring them together!

She found a comfortable rock and sat down, lifting her face to the mild warmth of the late afternoon sun. A thousand dreamy thoughts filled her head. When she finally noticed that the sun was on a definite downward track, she reluctantly got up to begin the rest of the walk home.

But something stopped her before she even got started. The silence, perhaps. It was unnaturally quiet. And then, as she puzzled at the stillness, she felt a sudden sensation of warmth encircle her, embracing her in a way that reminded her of the comfort of her mother's arms. The sensation was sweeter and more comforting than she had ever imagined a feeling could be. It rooted her to the spot; she could not have moved even if she'd wanted to.

She turned, searching for what could have caused the warmth and found the reason—the shimmering form of what could only be an angel stood before her. Without thought she sank to her knees.

A light, rapturous music danced about her—the air seemed to quiver with its gladness. The fields and trees were bathed in the light, consecrated by the holy being's presence. He was beautiful, glowing, powerful, and Mary was both awed and afraid. What could it mean?

"Greetings, favored one; the Lord is with you. Do not be afraid, Mary, for you have found favor with God."

Favored one! Mary gazed at the angel in wonder. What had she done to deserve the favor of God? The Lord was with her, the angel said!

His next words startled her even more:

"For you will conceive in your womb and bear a son," he said, his voice at the same time both gentle and forceful. "You shall call him Jesus. He will be great, and will be called the Son of the Most High; and the Lord God will give him the throne of his father David; and he will reign over the house of Jacob forever; and his kingdom will have no end."

A rush of warmth came over Mary, and she knew. She knew. Any Jewish girl would have known what the angel's words meant: this child he spoke of was the Messiah. The long-awaited Messiah who had been promised from ages past. She, Mary, was chosen to be mother to the Son of God!

Fear entered her heart, but only for a moment, replaced almost before it began with a sense of peace, warmth and love as the Spirit of God gave her gentle comfort.

"But how?" she asked in wonder. "How can this be, since I am a virgin?"

The angel smiled, and when he spoke, his voice was as vast and mighty as the ocean and as gentle as a baby's laugh.

"The Holy Spirit will come upon you, and the power of the Most High will overshadow you; and for that reason the Holy Child shall be called the Son of God."

Mary bowed her head as tears, unbidden, came to her eyes. To be so chosen, so honored, so loved! Unfathomable wonder, inexpressible joy!

Tears spilled down her cheeks as the angel spoke again: "Your relative Elizabeth has also conceived a son in her old age, and she who was called barren is now in her sixth month."

Mary's heart jumped. Could it be? Her older cousin, Elizabeth, had wanted a child so badly for so long, but she had never been able to conceive. She was past the time for bearing children now. Yet Mary knew in her heart that what the angel said was true was true, and knew also that the news had been given to her as a sign and a comfort.

Once again the angel spoke, and his voice was so beautiful and mighty it almost hurt to hear his words: "For nothing, *nothing* is impossible with God."

Nothing! God, all powerful, all knowing, all loving, had chosen to send his Son to earth—and it would be through her, Mary, a humble Jewish girl.

She looked at the angel, her eyes still misting with tears, then bowed her head. "I am the bondservant of the Lord. May it be done to me as you have said." The words came from the depths of her soul, and she meant them with all her heart.

The angel smiled, and then disappeared in a grand blaze of glorious light. Instantly another light, stronger and brighter, poured over and through Mary, surrounding her, dancing through her, filling her. Unspeakable joy! Closing her eyes, she stilled herself before the presence of God and worshipped as the miracle was begun.

It was dark when I finally walked home that evening. The fields and trees that had borne silent witness to a miracle were as peaceful and beautiful as they had always been, and I almost found it hard to believe that my life had been so changed. But I knew it had.

As my steps neared home, I began to hurry; I had so much to tell! Then I heard my mother's voice come anxiously over the cool wind: "Mary! Mary, where are you?"

"Here, Mother, I'm coming!"

I ran the last short distance up the hill, panting for breath and eager to share my news, but stopped still when I saw my mother's shocked face. I realized that some of the light from the angel must have clung to me.

"Mother, I have such wonderful news! I can't wait to tell you and Father." I cried, the eagerness and wonder in my heart bursting to be shared.

She followed me inside, and then quickly sent the children to the back room. The look on her face, and on my father's, too, told me they didn't know what to think. Before they had even sat down, I began my story, telling them everything that had happened to me, reliving it in my mind. I was so happy, so amazed, so wor-shipful that the words poured out of me.

But when I reached the end of my narrative and saw how it had affected them, I was brought quickly back to grim reality. Fear and doubt were written all over their faces.

"Mary," my father began awkwardly, "have you had a dream, a vision? I believe that something amaz-ing must have happened to you—but bear the Messiah?"

I stared at him. Was it possible my parents wouldn't believe me? Didn't believe me? I had been so caught up in the beauty, the glory, the light of God that I had never thought anyone might not believe me, and now I tasted for the first time the doubt that still sometimes haunts me.

I begged them to understand, to believe that it had really happened, that even as I spoke, the Holy Child was growing in me. But I saw their faces become more and more confused, and I began to see that they truly didn't believe me.

"Mary," my mother stopped me. "This story is...incredible, to say the least. Unbelievable. How could it be?" She hesitated, then blurted out, "Virgins don't have children, Mary! If something bad has happened to you, you must not be afraid to tell us—"

"Mother!" I interrupted, aghast at her words. "I am pure! There has been no sin in any of this—it's all from God, you must believe me!"

Desperately I looked from her to my father and back again. My heart fell. If anything, they looked even more doubtful.

When I climbed the stairs to my room that night, it was with a heavy heart. A thousand fears cut me and I felt as if I had been mortally wounded. My own parents didn't believe me.

Then I thought of Joseph, my betrothed. Joseph! What would he do? When it became clear I was with child, would he believe my explanation? We had been betrothed for almost a year, and our marriage was quickly approaching. Would he still accept me?

I knelt at my window, staring through tear-filled eyes at the stars, just beginning to shine in the sky. I had been so happy, so full of wonder at the news of the angel. But now I saw that before me lay many days of hardship. I only hoped that I would have the strength and willingness to endure.

The next day was even harder than the night before. When I came down from my room in the early morning, my mother greeted me brightly, questions in her eyes, and I knew she was hoping that what she considered my momentary insanity had been cured. When she found out otherwise, I saw the fear re-enter her eyes.

"Perhaps you have just imagined it, Mary. Time will tell." Her voice became brusque. "Now go to your chores." She turned her back to me, brushing me off.

Yes, time would tell all. And when it told the truth, I could only hope my mother would believe it.

The next days and weeks were filled with the usual rounds of work, interspersed with times of fun but shadowed with tension. I knew my parents were watching me closely. Soon, they would have to watch me no more, for even if they could not see the baby yet, I knew from the changes in my body that I was indeed bearing a child.

Those days were some of the most sorrowful I have ever known. In the first moments of supreme wonder and excitement I had experienced with the angel, I had thought that serving God in this way would be more joyful than I could imagine. But it was becoming increasingly clear that serving God would bring more hardship and pain than I had ever thought, and I cried out to God, begging him to help me stay faithful and soft toward him. I knew that my heart could easily be closed by bitterness and sorrow.

One of the things that most hurt me was the new distance I felt between my mother and me. We had always been so close, laughing together, working together, loving the same things and dreaming of the day when I, too, would have a home and children. Now the old camaraderie was gone, and though I knew she still loved me, I mourned for our lost friendship.

Finally the day came when I had to tell Joseph that I was with child. We met in our usual trysting spot, a secret place I treasured for its wonderful memories.

But on that day, it became a place of hurt and anger. I will never forget the shocked stare in Joseph's eyes when I told him. I tried to recreate the light of the angel and tell him all about my amazing experience, but when I spoke those four words, "I am with child," it was as if he forgot everything that had come before.

Rising from the rock where he sat beside me, he slammed his fist against a tree and let out a strangled cry. Then he rose, nursing his injured hand, and paced for a moment before turning to me with blazing fire in his gaze.

But his anger quickly turned to hurt. Tears formed in his eyes. "Mary, how could you do this? How could you do this? How could you lie to me when I have loved you so much? The least you could do is tell me the truth—not some fanciful story."

Before I could answer, he fled.

"Joseph!" I called after him. "Please! You must listen to me, you must believe me!"

He didn't stop. Sinking to the ground, my face in my hands, I wept, and for many hours I could not find the strength to move.

By the time Mary finally made her way home that night, she had resolved to visit Elizabeth. Maybe, because her cousin also carried a holy child, she would understand what Mary was going through. And if she went away, it would give Joseph time to sort out his thoughts, Mary told herself.

Her parents quickly agreed to the plan, perhaps hoping that being in the home of the priest Zachariah and his upright wife would bring about their daughter's repentance—or cure her of whatever it was that had come over her.

Those three months were the best Mary had ever known. Elizabeth instantly recognized her as the mother of the Messiah, and the baby in her womb leapt for joy, recognizing the holy baby in Mary's womb.

For a few precious months at least, she was in a place of peace, and the doubt and fear for the moment were gone. But all too soon her sojourn was over, and she had to return to her home in Nazareth.

She was showing now—not enough to be always obvious, but enough to raise the eyebrows and indignation of every person in her community. But armed with the assurance and peace she had found in her long talks with Elizabeth and her husband, Mary stood strong against the town's unspoken criticism. She reminded herself, just as Zachariah had reminded her, of the way God had been faithful to his people throughout history. Would he not be faithful to her now?

She needed her newfound strength, for when she returned and saw Joseph again, he coldly, but not unkindly told her he was going to divorce her. Once again, Mary wept.

Though Joseph went quietly to the elders of the village for his divorce, not wanting to disgrace Mary publicly, the news got out anyway. The next days were terrible. The townspeople criticized her openly. Friends stopped greeting her on the street, and people she had known all her life refused to talk to her.

Even Mary's best friend turned away from her. Not only did Hannah's parents make it clear that she was no longer welcome in their home, but Hannah herself refused to visit her or speak to her.

So Mary continued on in the midst of overwhelming rejection. She tried to be faithful, tried to remember the words of the angel, tried to keep true to her vow to God. But sometimes the discouragement felt unbearable.

One quiet night, Mary crept out of the house and made her way to the place where the angel had come to her. The night was as still as that other night had been, and when Mary knelt in the same place she had knelt before, her quiet sobs made the only noise in the evening fields.

She was more dejected than she ever had been. For an hour, she poured her heart out to God, sometimes simply crying, knowing he could read her tears. When she was silent again she prayed that God would give her strength and help her stay true to her vow, even in the face of so much pain.

She was just about to go back to the house, when suddenly she heard the sound of labored breathing and then her name:

"Mary! Mary, where are you? Come out to me!"

Joseph! What was he doing here?

Hurrying in the direction of the voice, she saw him running toward her. "Joseph?" she called.

A moment later, without warning, Joseph grabbed her up and swung her around, then hugged her close.

Tears stung Mary's eyes. She didn't know why, but she knew Joseph wanted her again. She knew—oh joy!—that he loved her.

When he let her go and dropped to one knee with her hand still in his, her eyes grew wide.

"Mary," he said, gazing at her with pleading eyes, "sweetest Mary, please forgive me. Forgive me for ever rejecting you. I was so wrong! I should never have doubted you—you have always been the most truthful, loving person I know. Please, forgive me!"

Unable to speak, Mary reached down to wipe a tear from his cheek and then dropped to her knees to face him.

"Mary," he said, "an angel has come to me, just the way he came to you. I know now that the child you bear is from God. And Mary—I truly believe that God chose you for all the reasons that I love you: your sweetness, your willingness to help, your love. I will never doubt you again. I love you, Mary. I want you to be my wife."

When Joseph spoke those wonderful words, it was as if he poured a healing oil over the wounds in my heart. Later that night, after he took me home and spoke with my parents, I knelt again at my window. Remembering the night of the angel's visit, when I had knelt in the same place, I closed my eyes and took a deep breath.

If I had known then what hardship lay ahead, I'm not sure what I would have done. But God carried me through every heartache and over every obstacle. And now, with my loving Joseph at my side, I hold my baby Jesus in my arms, Jesus, the Son of the Most High. What greater gift of love could God ever bestow?"

This story is taken from Matthew 1:18-25 & Luke 1:26-56

Reflections

Pulling my jacket close around me, I stepped out onto the porch. It was frigid that night in our mountains, and I knew I was crazy to be out in the subzero weather. But if I stayed inside for one more instant, I was sure I would go mad! The walls of the house were closing in on me, and I had to escape for at least a few minutes.

Earlier that day, I had found out about a contract offer on this book, my very first! But my excitement had quickly worn thin when I realized I had no one with whom I could share my good news. I had not a single friend nearby to help me celebrate.

I was so lonely! Where were the friends I longed for? Why wasn't God bringing friends my way? I felt almost as if he were purposely keeping them out of my life.

As I stood there in the cold, pondering and trying to pray, a new realization came upon me: *the standards my family and I held separated us from other people.*

I don't think I had ever realized that the values my family held made it hard for me to find a kindred spirit. Everything we did and held dear seemed so natural to me, and because I had never suffered for my beliefs, I had never called them into question. But now I was faced with the reality that I would have to suffer for what I believed was right. That was when it started feeling hard to keep being faithful.

I think there comes a time in every Christian's life when you have to count the cost of following Christ, when your vow of faith is tested by suffering. It is at that point, when the pain is great and a person still chooses to follow God that true faith comes into play.

I see that kind of faith in Mary's life. Before I really studied her life, I saw her as an almost perfect girl—she must have been, I thought, for God to have chosen her. But I believe now he chose her not because she was perfect, but because she was willing. Not just willing to carry his Son, but willing to go through the pain and loneliness she would have to suffer and still believe that God was faithful.

Mary suffered greatly. She was a sweet, young Jewish girl, engaged to be married and ready to live a normal life, when the angel came and told her she had been chosen to bear the Son of God. Can you imagine? She must have been terrified. No human had ever been in such close contact with God.

Her whole world was turned upside down by the presence of the holy child in her womb. But I'm sure most of the people in her family and village thought the baby anything but holy. She must have endured mountains of criticism, perhaps the threat of being stoned for adultery, certainly the shame of Joseph's intent to divorce her. After that there were long journeys, periods of homelessness, the birth of her baby in a strange place and so much more.

It must have been easy for her to say "yes" to God at first, when the glory of the angel shone in front of her. What I think is amazing is that when she was faced with rejection, she chose to accept God's plan for her. When faced with sorrow, she tried to take joy in her Lord. When faced with hardship, she was willing to endure for the sake of God.

Her true willingness is shown by the fact that she kept on, when the glow of the angel was no longer surrounding her.

So often in my life I will be inspired to a new goal or idea, but as soon as the excitement wears off and harsh reality steps in, I turn back, remembering only the hardship. With the enthusiasm for a new cause in my heart, it is easy to be willing, to say "yes" to God, but when criticism and hardship take the excitement away, I find my willingness disappearing.

As Christians, if we are determined to follow Christ we will bear the pain of suffering. Our faith will be tested, just like Mary's was. But if we can look ahead, keep our eyes on Jesus, remember the joy of heaven that will someday come—if we can keep on being faithful, God will use us in wonderful ways.

When I went inside that night, my cheeks may have been cold, but my heart was warm again. I would not change one thing about what I believed, and though it would be hard, I knew that with God's help I would make it. Like Mary, I am God's bondservant, willing to follow wherever he leads.

Read: 2 Timothy 3:12a

Reflect:

Every person who follows God will suffer and be persecuted. The wonderful thing is that when we suffer, we share in the sufferings of Christ and begin to know him more and depend on him alone. Why do you think that every Christian must suffer? In what way does this bring us closer to God? Do you think God can use someone who isn't willing to suffer? Are you willing to suffer?

Read: John 16:33

Reflect:

Why did Jesus "tell them these things"? What can we expect from the world? Will we ever "fit in" to the world? What has Jesus overcome?

Read: Philippians 3:8-10

Reflect:

What does Paul consider a loss? What does he gain in the losing of it? What does Paul want to know more than anything else in the world? What are "all things" to you?

Read: Hebrews 12:1-3

Reflect:

To what does Paul compare the Christian life? How are we to run this race even in the face of discouragement? Who is the example to whom we look for encouragement?

Journey Journal

Chapter 8
The Refiner's Fire

I remember so well the day I left home, the home of my whole life. For days I had been preparing myself for the parting. But when the time came, all my resolve to be brave and strong melted away, and I felt as if my heart was about to break. Tears streaming down my face, I held my mother in one last long embrace, trying to impress on my memory forever the dear face and soft touch that was so precious to me.

A cold spring wind whipped around us. For a moment, I felt as if I were a child again, wrapped in the security of my mother's arms where nothing could ever hurt me. But in an instant the feeling was gone, and I was left with the bleak reality that this was truly goodbye.

My swollen stomach, pressing against my mother as she held me, formed a wall between us. The child I bore separated me from my mother as surely as he separated me from everything and everyone else.

With a last, loving kiss, I pulled myself away and allowed Joseph to set me on the donkey.

I knew we had to go. A census had been called, and Joseph had to journey to Bethlehem to be registered. Of course I must go with him. But leaving now, when my time was so near and my parents were still struggling with my pregnancy, would not have been my choice. I wondered at God's timing. Why did this have to happen now?

From my seat on the donkey I took one last look around at the fields I had worked with my parents, the warm house my father had built, the houses of neighbors who had known me since I was a babe in my mother's arms. I wished this spring storm had not blown in overnight; the gray skies and cold wind robbed the scene of the color and warmth I wanted to take away in my memories.

Finally my eyes turned to my family, my parents and my brothers and sisters huddled together in front of the house. My parents' faces were anxious and drawn. I looked at them pityingly. I knew how hard it was for them, without the assurance of God's will in their hearts, to let me go. "I love you—all of you—so much," I said. My voice sounded small and fragile in the cold air.

"Take care of yourself, my Mary," my mother said quietly, stepping forward and laying a hand on my face. "May God go with you."

"He will, Mother. Truly, he is always with me, for I am walking the road he would have me walk."

Mother looked up at me and sighed, and my heart ached with that sigh. She still could not believe. It broke my heart to think of leaving her so hopeless.

I felt Joseph's hand on my arm. "It's time to go," he said.

And it was. I knew that God was leading me, rather than taking me, from this loved place, but the pain of parting was so much greater than I had anticipated, the prospect of seeing my family again anytime soon so small.

With a wind-blown kiss to my parents and each of my sisters and brothers, I steadied myself for a long ride as the donkey began to plod ahead. Slowly, my family's forms grew smaller, and I tried to keep the tears from spilling onto my cheeks as everything familiar was swallowed up in the gray mists.

As we left the village, I saw the face of my best friend peering out a window of her home. Tears streamed down her face, but when she saw that I saw her, she turned away, refusing even to say goodbye. Even she had rejected me when it became known I was carrying a child, and I felt as though a knife had been stabbed through my heart.

Finally, the little town was lost in the mist behind us, and all I could see was the road stretching out in front of us—a long road leading to an uncertain future. I felt more desolate than I had ever felt. Why did following God have to be so hard?

It had been a week—seven days of constant travel on rutted dirt roads, with only short rests huddled on the ground near a campfire during the chill nights. The weight of physical exhaustion lay heavily on Mary, making the sense of sadness in her heart even more difficult to bear.

For several nights now, she had been unable to sleep, driven from her bed next to the fire by her restlessness and discouragement. She felt as if God had forgotten her. She had committed to serving him; she was following his leading—so why did she feel so alone and lost? Where was the peace and joy he promised his children?

Even during the days she felt alone. She had always loved the outdoors, but now she found no joy in the cool breeze or the wide, open fields or the vast sky with its parade of clouds. Where was the joy of her Lord? For that matter, where was God?

She rode in silence, walking every now and then to work out the cramps in her legs, feeling little except the pain in her heart. How much longer could she go on like this?

One evening after a long day on the dusty road, they stopped to take shelter under a grove of sturdy trees. Joseph scraped and blew to get a fire crackling while Mary rummaged through their bags, pulling out blankets and bread for their supper.

As night crept quietly through the valley and the sky faded into an ocean of darkness awash with stars, Mary left Joseph sitting by the fire and wandered away from the shelter of the trees to the open field. Dark—it was so dark. She shivered and pulled her shawl closer around her, hugging her shoulders.

All she could see and all she could feel was darkness. Where was God? If only she could see evidence of his love!

Reaching down, her hands caressed her growing stomach, and she felt suddenly anxious. It was because of her willingness to carry this holy child that so much hardship had befallen her. "God, are you out there?" she murmured. "Do you care how I feel?"

For almost half an hour she stood in the darkness, asking for God's help, waiting for some sign of his love, feeling guilty for her sense of despair but helpless to do anything about it.

Suddenly warm arms went around her. Joseph.

Putting her hands over his, Mary leaned against her husband and felt comforted. They stood in silence for a few calm moments, then she turned to him with wistful eyes.

"I wonder what they're doing at home tonight. Maybe mother is cooking supper or Father is playing with the children. I can picture it so clearly, but they all seem so far away."

A lump rose in Mary's throat, and she closed her eyes for a moment. Two small tears coursed down her cheeks. "Joseph, it seems that this business of following God is very hard. Do you think I'll ever feel happy and free again? It doesn't seem fair that I should follow God and still suffer, but I don't know how to think about it all—I just don't know."

With a timid glance at her husband again, she saw Joseph looking at her with troubled eyes. She started to say something, but stopped as he began to speak.

"Mary, I know how hard these weeks have been on you. I have felt your sorrow right along with you. But do you know, just this evening as I sat at the fire, I remembered a song you used to sing. I think you said it was the lullaby your mother rocked you to sleep with every night when you were a baby. Do you remember?"

Joseph began to hum the tune softly, and Mary smiled at the familiar words:

"The nighttime will last for just a while,
But gladness will come in the morning."

She was silent for a few moments, thinking of the song, remembering the many cozy evenings she had spent in her mother's arms. She felt better with Joseph's comforting arms around her and the precious lullaby in her heart.

"Mary," Joseph broke the sweet silence, "I think everything will be just as the song says. The nighttime, the darkness will last for a while, but I really believe that someday—soon, I hope—the morning will come. Just keep waiting for the morning, Mary. Just keep waiting for the morning."

Joseph fell silent. Craning her neck around to see him, Mary saw his eyes sweeping the sky. Looking up, she, too, saw the millions of stars sparkling above them, and a few minutes later when they turned back to their little camp, she felt that some light was beginning to sparkle again in her heart.

She lay silently beside Joseph, the campfire casting its warmth around her, thinking about what her husband had said. Her heart was still heavy with longing for her family, with the sorrow of hurting them and losing so many dear friends, but she knew that God was good; she would just have to think of this time in her life as the night in her journey.

Lifting her eyes to the sky again, Mary saw the thousands of stars shining so beautifully above her. Suddenly she gasped and almost laughed. A surprising and sweet little thought had come to her head. Though she knew that the morning in her heart would be longer in coming, there were still stars to light her night, just as the stars sparkled above her now in the darkness.

Joseph loved her—that was the brightest star. Then there was Elizabeth's understanding, the baby in her womb, the sweet sense of peace that sometimes flooded her heart—all of these things lit the way that seemed so dark to her now.

Closing her eyes, Mary made a silent vow to God. She knew now, supposed she had known all along, that morning would come. And all along the way, if she would just remember to turn her gaze heavenward, she would find stars in her life.

Her eyes closed, and for the first time in days, her sleep was peaceful.

After that night under the stars, I felt my heart slowly begin to heal. I watched for the stars in my life and waited for morning to come, and watching and waiting comforted me.

The days that followed were a blur of new sights, sounds and colors, and when we finally reached Bethlehem, I was more relieved than I could say.

Joseph had a distant relative in Bethlehem, and we sought him out. He had not seen Joseph's family for so long that he was overjoyed to welcome us, and though he had no room for us in the house, he let us stay in the shed out back.

We had been there only a day when I felt the first pains of labor. I marveled at God's timing, and counted yet another star in my life. It was cold the night I gave birth to my baby. For hours I struggled, the pain so great I thought I would die. Joseph never left my side, refusing to leave even after the midwife came. But still the delivery was difficult, and I was tempted to despair as my physical pain opened up all the old sadness. The darkness hovered over me like a blanket.

Then it was over, and in my arms I wonderingly held a miracle. I looked into my baby's eyes, held him close and felt his soft breathing, and remembered all at once that he was the Son of God. The Son of God! All my pain and sadness fled in the light of the wonder, gratitude and joy I felt as I held my baby—a joy more complete than any I had ever imagined. Morning had finally come.

I will never forget the delight, the utter contentment, of holding my baby and knowing that I held God's Son. Yet I loved him not only as the holy child he was, but also as my precious son, born from my body. I loved him with all the tenderness a mother can give.

I spent hours nursing him, holding him, talking to him, marveling at the miracle that had brought him to my arms. I tasted again of the joy and blessing of my God. I was able once again to praise him for his faithfulness, to see his goodness in my life.

For a month more we lived in the cramped, but cozy stable, Joseph supporting us with odd carpentry jobs and I mothering my baby boy.

As I looked back at the weeks before the birth of my baby, I remembered the darkness, and thanked God that he had brought about my morning. But I was beginning to understand that suffering comes with the blessing of being chosen by God, but God always provides stars in the lives of those who serve him. And I knew that I would always follow him, even when night came again.

When forty days had passed, the time came for us to travel to Jerusalem and offer a sacrifice to the Lord, dedicating our firstborn son to him according to the Law. I looked forward to being in the temple; in a way, I felt that I would be rededicating myself to God as well as dedicating Jesus.

And so, early one morning, our little family packed everything we owned and began yet another journey, this time to the holy city of Jerusalem.

Finally the day came, and I walked into the awesome glory of the temple, marveling at the white pillars, intricate tapestries, and gold tools of the priests.

When it was time for the sacrifice, I watched as the priest took up the two doves, symbols of a peace offering to God. I closed my eyes, holding my little baby boy tightly against me. In my heart, as the priest made the offering to God, I made an offering, too. I had given myself wholly to God before, promising to always follow him no matter what. But I had been greatly tested, by the sorrow and rejection because of my commitment, and I had been tempted at times to fall away in despair.

But I understood now what it meant to follow God, and I wanted to re-dedicate myself to God, giving myself to him regardless of what my choice brought, and in my heart I knew he was pleased.

Cuddling my baby close against me, I whispered to him, describing the great house of his Father in which we stood, telling him of the faithfulness of God. At that moment, I felt a gentle hand touch my arm, and turning, I beheld an old, wizened man, a priest. He was much like many of the other priests in the temple, but I will never forget the excitement on his face.

Without further introduction, he told me that his name was Simeon, and he had come to see Jesus. Somehow this man knew that the tiny baby I held was the Messiah, and he had come to worship him. With tears in my eyes, I handed Jesus to him and watched in joy as he embraced the baby in his arms, kissed him, prophesied over him. It was one of the most beautiful sights I have ever seen.

In that moment, God's faithfulness to me was confirmed. What a miracle, that out of the thousands of families who passed through the temple every day, Simeon would recognize my baby as the Messiah!

Suddenly the old priest turned to me with urgency in his voice. "This child will cause the rise and fall of many in Israel," he said. A tender sadness filled his eyes as he gazed at Jesus, but turning back to me with love and almost pity in his old eyes, he added, "And a sword will pierce your own heart, too."

It was as if I could feel the sword in my heart as he said it. I knew it well; hadn't it already pierced my heart horribly? Kissing Jesus' soft forehead one more time, Simeon handed him back to me, reaching up to pat my arm. With one last glance for Jesus, and a smile for me, he was gone. But his words had touched me, and I knew that I would never be the same again.

Later that night, as we sat around the fire, I thought of the miracle this day had unfolded. How encouraging it was to realize that others knew my baby as the Messiah, and how wonderful God had been to arrange it! I thought of the prophecy Simeon had made over Jesus and wondered what the next years would bring. Then I remembered Simeon's words about a sword piercing my heart.

I knew of that sword already—the sword of suffering. In the great night that I had journeyed in the last months of my pregnancy, I had felt its sharp edge in my soul. But just as surely as the sword and the darkness had wounded me, so had the light and love of God's faithfulness surrounded me and comforted me. Even in the deepest darkness, the stars of love in my life had shone bright. I had finally discovered the meaning of my mother's sweet song, and I knew that even if night overtook me again, morning would come.

And I would wait for it. God had proven himself to be faithful and loving, and though I knew I would struggle many more times in my life, I also knew that God never leaves his children alone, they just have to keep their eyes open to the stars he brings into their lives.

Leaving the fire, I walked out into the field and gazed up at the stars, admiring them and enjoying the cold breeze against my face.

I thought again of the words I had spoken to the angel when he brought me the incredible news that I was to bear the son of God: I am the bondservant of the Lord; may it be done to me as you have said. At the time, my vow to the Lord was heartfelt but untested. Now I knew well the darkness of night and the pain of suffering. Now, lifting my face to the night sky, I spoke my vow again. This time my words were tried and true, tested by the night and the sword and made holy by the love and joy of the morning:

"I am the bondservant of the Lord; may it be done to me as you have said."

And so it was.

This story is taken from Luke 2:1-35

Reflections

I stepped into the living room and sat down on the couch, pulling a blanket around my shoulders. It was evening, dark and cool, with the first stars just beginning to shine. I watched the shadows grow longer, saw the flicker of the fire. Usually I loved a quiet evening with a book and fire, and I tried to enjoy it now. But I couldn't. Tonight it was too silent, and a sense of despair had been building in me all day. I was tired, weary, and depressed.

I often have times when I feel restless, discouraged and weary, and loneliness doesn't help those feelings. But this time I was more down than usual. The last two months had been extra busy, and I was exhausted—weary of being diligent. It didn't seem that I had anything to look forward to, no excitement, no friends with whom I could have some fun. In my heart, I knew I had neglected to spend time with the Lord, but to tell the truth, I was beginning to feel that he didn't care about me.

That made me feel very unspiritual, which made matters worse. I felt guilty about my depression and discouraged that I couldn't make myself feel better by praying and simply "trusting God." But in my time of loneliness and weariness, I needed something more, something to warm the cold in my heart.

Night came in earnest as I sat in front of the fire, and the stars shone more brightly than ever. I felt a small hand on my shoulder, and a little someone kissed me on the cheek. "Hi Sabah," said my sweet six-year old sister, using her babyhood name for me. "We've come to watch the fire with you." And with that, she and Mom sat down beside me.

I felt instantly comforted to have my loved ones near me. And as we sat, talking of little things and simply enjoying each other's company, the coldness in my heart began to melt

Throughout our soup-and-bread dinner and family reading time, I grew happier and happier. Maybe life wasn't so bad after all.

Later that night as I lay in bed with Joy snuggled close against me, the moon glowing gently through the window, I thought about what it was that had caused me to feel so much better. I realized that it was in the love of my family and the security of our home that I was comforted. I took pleasure from our cozy fireside times and long talks with my mom. I found joy in our evening meals and the hugs of my siblings.

A verse suddenly came to mind: "Every good and perfect gift is from above" (James 1:17).

All of the gifts in my life—my family, our home, the beauty of nature—all were from God. Earlier I had questioned if he really cared for me, but now I saw evidences of his love all around me. Even when I was surrounded by darkness, God had taken care to place shining stars in my life, to assure me of his love.

God knew that I would sometimes be lonely, and so he gave me a good family to love and encourage me when I need it. He knew I would sometimes be discouraged and wonder if he really was there, so he gave me wildflowers, blue skies and mountains to assure me of his presence. He knew I would sometimes feel insecure, so he gave me a warm, loving home where I know I am safe when life seems overwhelming.

There were many times in Mary's life, too, when I know she felt discouraged, lonely and weary. But she was able to see, eventually, that God really did care for her. She found joy in her child, comfort in Joseph's integrity and faithful love, joy and assurance in Simeon's prophecy. And I know she must have seen God's beauty in her nights under the stars. She learned to look around her for evidences of God's love in the small things of life, and there she found comfort.

If we can remember to look for God's love, and count the stars in our lives even in the midst of hardship, it will make our journey so much easier. I know I will still feel lonely and down at times, but God in his mercy has surrounded me with things in which I find comfort. And in those things I see his love.

Looking back, I can't say that knowing all this has made my down times any easier, but I am learning to trust God with them and take joy from his gifts of love and comfort. When I feel despondency coming on, I hurry to hug Joy, take a long walk in the mountains or have a heart talk with Mom—all the while taking comfort in the stars of my life, remembering that they are a gift from my loving Father.

Read: James 1:17

Reflect:

Who is the giver of every perfect gift? What are the perfect gifts in your life? Have you thanked God for them and remembered to count them among your blessings even when you're down? Is there any shadow in God? Are you perfectly sure of his love for you?

Read: Isaiah 51:12a

Reflect:

Who is the one who comforts us in our time of need? What does this say about God's will and attitude towards us? What gifts has God given you that bring you comfort in your time of darkness?

Read: 1 Thessalonians 5:16-18

Reflect:

What are we to always be? What are we to continually do? Why do you think God wants us to give thanks in everything, and how does this apply to the down times in life? What are some things for which you can be thankful?

Read: Psalm 34:8

Reflect:

Do you think the Lord's goodness is tangible in your life, and if so, how? What will we find when we take refuge in God? How does this apply to finding his joy in the dark times of life?

Journey Journal

Chapter 9
Adapting to Change

"*Oh no, not again,* Lord," *I said under my breath.*

It was the middle of the night, and moments before I had wakened to my husband whispering in my ear. Now everything was quiet except for the few peaceful sounds of a cricket and the wind outside our window. "What is it, Joseph?"

"Mary, I've had a dream."

I turned over to see him with a deep sigh. I knew what those words meant: something in my life was about to change drastically.

I had been expecting something like this—and dreading it as well. For the first time in months I felt safe and secure. After Jesus was born, Joseph found some carpentry work around Bethlehem, and we were happily settled in a small house on the outskirts of town.

Just two days before, the day that marked six months in our new home, we'd had an incredible visit from three kings from the East—wise men, they called themselves. They had followed a star sent from God, they said, right to our very door, and they had come to worship the new King as they called Jesus. Halfway across the world, God had told three men of the birth of his Son, and they had come to worship! I was awed and thankful.

They brought gifts with them, costly gifts: gold, frankincense and myrrh, treasures that should belong to a king. But my Jesus was a King.

The first thing we did with the treasure was use a small part to pay our debt on the house. It was such a relief to me to finally have a secure home for my family, and I reveled in the comfort of having my own domain. I loved making it cozy and warm, and cooking for the three of us, and having a place and the time to play with my baby and look after him in peace.

I was so thankful to God for finding us this comfortable house, and I felt that after having traveled so far from my own precious home, God had made a home for me right where we were. I loved it—but now, God had sent Joseph a dream, and everything was about to change.

I looked him squarely in the eye by the light of the moon, steeling myself for the worst.

"What are we to do Joseph? What does God want us to do?"

For a moment, I felt his eyes on me in the darkness, and his hand covered mine. He was so sweet, but this worried me a little. What was the news?

"Don't worry dear," I said, "with God's help and your love I can do anything. But just what is this anything we're supposed to do?"

He hesitated, and I nudged him gently.

"We're moving to Egypt."

I was stunned. Egypt? Of all the places in the world I didn't want to go, Egypt was the first! Egypt, where people hated Jews and still looked on us as slaves. Egypt—hot, dry, foreign. Why, the Egyptians worshiped animals! I stared at my husband in amazement. Was it really true?

"It's true, Mary," Joseph said, as if answering my thoughts. "God wants us to go to Egypt for the safety of our child. There are those here who want to kill him."

"Oh, Joseph," I groaned miserably, "I will do anything to keep Jesus safe, but Egypt, of all places! I just don't understand, why now when we're so settled?"

Joseph didn't answer, probably because he had no answer. I looked around my bedroom, and through the door into the front room beyond. Those rooms had become home to me, and I already missed the peace of their walls.

Closing my eyes and trying to swallow the insistent ache in my throat, I took a deep breath and asked the next dreaded question:

"When are we to go?"

He hesitated. "I think we are to go tonight."

"Tonight!"

My jaw dropped. I would have thought we would have at least a few days to pack and prepare. A few more days of peace, a few more moments of joy in the midst of work, a few more days of security. I couldn't believe I had to leave everything right at that minute!

Hearing my sigh of desperation, Joseph hastened to explain. "Mary, when the wise men came just the other day, do you remember they mentioned going to Herod's palace first? As you know, they were warned in a dream not to go back that way, and now I know for certain why: Herod is out to kill Jesus. Jerusalem is barely a good day's walk from here. The soldiers could be here by morning. We have to leave tonight—please. Mary, can't you see that?"

I nodded, feeling defeated. When God has planned it, what will be will be. I knew yet again that he was asking me to give up everything to follow him. It seemed to me that following God involved a lot of packing.

"All right, Joseph," I said. "Let's go. You pack up your tools and whatever furniture you think we can take with us, and I'll pack all the other goods. Don't wake Jesus until the last."

So it was done. Within two hours we had packed everything we could into our old wooden cart. With an aching heart, I pulled my sturdy door shut for the last time, stopping first to take a last glance around the cozy rooms that I so loved. I climbed up beside Joseph, holding tight to my seat as our faithful donkey once again began to plod ahead.

With longing in my heart, I looked back at our home, barely perceptible now in the darkness. My vision blurred with tears. Yet again, it was time to go.

Memphis, a bustling city on the Nile delta, among other things, was dirty. Dirty, hot, dusty, foreign—in short, all the things Mary had known it would be.

They arrived in the huge Egyptian city after two weeks of travel on dusty, rutted roads. Pushing her cloak back from her head, Mary looked around her. The busy city streets overflowed with people, shops and animals. Taking a deep breath, she gave Joseph a brave smile as he guided the donkey through the crowd.

It had been a fairly easy journey as journeys go, but Mary was tired. Yet she was also much happier than when she had left Bethlehem. The first day, she had stewed over the suddenness with which the move had taken place; sometimes she had to wonder at the way God worked. To tell the truth, she was slightly irritated with God. After all, she had been willing to suffer to become the mother of God so it seemed as if he could at least provide a nice home in which she could raise his son! So far, six months was the longest they'd stayed anywhere. She was beginning to resent being constantly uprooted from every place she thought of as home. Serving God wasn't all it was cracked up to be.

The instant the thought had come to her mind, she felt guilty for it. Of course she wanted to serve God, and with all that was in her. When she had said "yes" to him, she had meant it for then and forevermore.

So, with a sigh, she had chosen to stop thinking about it. She would try to look forward with a positive mind to her new home in Egypt, though she was having a hard time finding anything positive about the whole idea.

She forced herself to remember all the blessings God had given her and to repeat over and over to herself the vow she had made to the angel, and it had helped. Though she was discouraged, she would hold true to that vow.

They spent their first days in Egypt finding a house, making a home out of the one they found and getting adjusted in general to life in a foreign land. They made their home in the middle of the city, near the shop where Joseph worked as an assistant carpenter. His Egyptian employer had accepted him right away, for Joseph was very skilled at his work.

In her tiny house squeezed between two larger buildings, Mary struggled to make the bare room homelike. First she made simple white curtains for the windows. Then she found rugs for the floor. Before long, with her dishes stacked neatly by the fireplace, the room began to look like a home.

At first Mary found it hard to adjust to her new life. The noise of the city disturbed her, and it seemed that the other women purposely ignored her. She missed her life in Bethlehem the same way she had missed her life in her parents' house in the months after she first left home. She had had so many expectations of what God was going to do for her, and coming to Egypt had completely thrown her off track.

But she was learning to adjust, and adjust with grace, to her new surroundings. She had learned the lesson of trusting God, and once again put it into action.

It took many days before the Egyptian women came knocking on her door, but after awhile, her neighbors did come, timidly, hiding packages of bread or food under their linen dresses, and Mary saw friendship reflected in their dark eyes.

Soon, the growing little Jesus was romping on the floor with the other babies of the neighborhood, and with a few words and many gestures, Mary learned to communicate with the other women. She also found that a large community of Jews lived in the city, and it was so heartwarming to find someone with whom she could share her heart. She became close friends with many of the women. Happiness again filled her heart, and she marveled at the change.

When she thought about it though, she realized that she had been angry with God for disrupting her life yet again, resentful at being forced to move to Egypt. When she had made a conscious choice to let go of her anger, she had quickly come to see what her anger was all about. It came down to one word: pride. She was, after all, the mother of the Son of God. It just wasn't fair that she had to keep moving, keep adjusting to new places and new lives. God should be providing her with a mansion—or at the very least a nice house—in which to raise his Son. After all, she had been so faithful to follow him!

Somehow she had been able to see through her pride, to realize that following God required faith, grace and flexibility. She couldn't have set expectations about her life, and at the same time be truly free to follow God.

So she made what she could of their life in Egypt, learning more every day what it meant to trust, feeling more and more at peace. She knew that change was somewhere around the corner, and this time she would be ready for it. This time she would better trust God.

We lived in Egypt for five contented years before Joseph had another of his dreams. God had come to him in the night, but he had waited to tell me until he came home from his work that afternoon. I had stepped outside to enjoy the few wisps of a breeze that managed to float down between the taller buildings to cool the narrow streets.

A sky full of rolling clouds met my eyes, and I felt supremely happy as I stood silently against the wall of my house watching the people pass by and listening to the wind. Little Jesus—well, not so little anymore—ran out and caught at my skirts.

"Look at the pretty clouds, Mama," he cried happily, and I smiled as I watched him hop from one foot to the other in childish excitement. It still amazed me that he was the Son of God. The only time I really felt it was when I realized that he had never spoken angrily to Joseph or me, and that he was perfectly obedient. Other than that, he was a normal little boy, interested in bugs and dirt, with a long history of scraped knees.

"Here comes Daddy!" he squealed, and I looked up to see his father walking swiftly down the road. With a shouted hello, Joseph ran and caught Jesus up in his arms, swinging him around and around as Jesus shrieked in delight. Coming up with Jesus still hanging off his arm, he kissed me, and with his arm around my shoulders, the three of us made our way inside.

There was an air of excitement about him, and I could see a sparkle in his eyes as he watched me finish our evening meal and set the table. From time to time I looked at him and caught him watching me. Finally, when we were all seated around the table, he made the announcement I could tell he was bursting to make. He sought my eyes and held them.

"Mary, Jesus, God has told me what we are to do. We are moving again." Here he stopped, waiting, I suppose, to see our reactions. I looked at him eagerly, both excited and apprehensive. Where in the world would God take us next? Rome?

"Where, Joseph?" I begged.

"We are going back to Israel. To Judea!"

Jumping up, I ran to his chair and threw my arms around him. "Oh, Joseph! We're going home!"

Joining in on the fun, Jesus clapped his hands and banged his bowl on the table.

Tears came to my eyes, tears both of happiness and sadness. I had grown to love my Egyptian and Jewish neighbors, and our home here, though small, was happy. Who could tell what lay ahead?

But I remembered the resolution I had made when I first came to Egypt, that I would trust God with everything. We had been moved from place to place so many times, our lives disrupted and changed, yet each time God had been faithful to provide for us in every way. Perhaps I was finally learning to trust God, to adapt to the new places in which he put me.

I knew that I would have to accept the unexpected again as I traveled, and once again I would have to adapt to a new home. But I knew in my heart that this time, and ever after, I would not only adapt to, but embrace, the changes in my life, knowing they were from God.

When I went to sleep that night, I felt more at peace than I had ever been. I had finally learned that I could always trust in the wisdom and love of my tender Father. I was his maidservant, and he would never leave me.

"I love you Father," was my last thought before I fell asleep.

This story is taken from Matthew 2:1-23

Reflections

I am not flexible. It is a fact of my life, and anyone who knows me will confirm it. It's not that I'm so very scheduled; in fact, I can be a very fun and spontaneous person. Just don't throw a curveball at me. Don't upset my expectations.

Once I've set my mind on what I'm going to do, whether day-to-day, for a holiday or for anything else, it's set—and I mean in stone.

Unfortunately, my lifestyle is not at all conducive to set-in-stone expectations. In fact, between living in a big family, traveling, writing, schoolwork and visitors, there is rarely a moment that goes as planned.

My parents are speakers and writers, and I am following in their footsteps, so we travel fairly often. January through June is our busiest time. This past year was especially hectic because we had four big conferences and five book-fairs, plus friends visiting and any number of other things. I can still remember the exact moment I first realized what a very un-flexible person I am.

It was evening, the night before our second conference was to begin. It had been a full day, overflowing with last-minute preparations to make sure everything was perfect, plus plenty of laughter and fun with friends who were visiting. Despite the fun, I was tired, and I was looking forward to a quiet evening with my friend when Mom came over, and asked if I would drive her to the hotel, forty-five minutes away.

I'm tired, and I already have plans for tonight, I thought.

"Sure, Mom, if you need me too," I said. But I gave that "Sure, Mom" all the sighs and tiredness I could muster. The trip would take out my whole evening.

Before we left, I walked into the laundry room to take my khaki skirt—part of our conference "uniform"—out of the dryer. (The uniform for our conferences is khaki skirts or slacks with blue denim shirts.) To my dismay, I found that I had left my lipstick in my skirt pocket. I had no idea that one tube of lipstick could wreak such havoc! It was clear I would not only be taking my mom to the hotel that night, I would also be shopping for a new skirt. Did I mention that I hate shopping late at night?

Several minutes and four more unexpected happenings later, I was sitting on the stool at the kitchen counter, shoulders slumped, head in my hands, wanting to yell, "Too many curveballs!"

At that moment I felt a hand on my shoulder and heard Mom say gently—very gently—"Try to be just a little more flexible, honey." And with that I was left alone.

I sat up, furrowing my brows. Flexible? I had never thought about whether or not I was flexible. But with crushing realization, I saw that it was my whole problem. I was so like stone, you'd have to hit me with a hammer to move me! Bending was not my strength.

I think I began to understand, at that moment in the kitchen, that just being alive is sometimes hectic. And unless I figured out how to hit the curveballs that came my way, I was going to be miserable.

I also realized, to my embarrassment, that I was so set on getting my way, having my priorities and my expectations met, that I hadn't thought of anyone else. I hadn't thought of Mom, who was anxious to work on her speech, or Joy, who was going to be lonely with Mom gone for the night, or Dad, who had a million and one details to pull together before the conference.

In short, I considered my own needs as more important than anyone else's. I had become abominably prideful and selfish.

Not only that, but in my unwillingness to accept even the gentle curveballs of life, I was showing God that I wasn't ready to take any of the big curveballs that come with serving God in a fallen world. I wasn't accepting that everything in my life was from his hand.

That night I finally saw my inflexibility and the cause of it, and I began working to change.

Later on, as I was reading my Bible, I flipped through Mary's story, and it struck me how many times she was moved, uprooted, and forced to live in uncertainty. She had to be very flexible, and something tells me it wasn't always easy.

Mary's humility and willingness played a key role in helping her to adjust and adapt with grace to her surroundings. She learned to understand that every unexpected thing that came into her life was from the Lord, and she learned to trust him. Inflexibility often shows pride and a lack of trust in God.

Since looking at myself honestly that night, I'm learning to trust, to bend. Slowly but surely, I'm actually becoming more flexible. I've learned to accept the curveballs as from God's hand, and as often as I can, I try to reach at least first base with them. And every once in a while I get a home run, and I can almost hear God cheering.

Read: Proverbs 19:21

Reflect:

What word is used to describe the number of plans a man makes? What does that say about us? Whose purpose will always prevail in the end? Do you truly believe that God's plans are best for you? What is an area in your life that could use some trust and flexibility?

Read: 2 Corinthians 5:7

Reflect:

How are we to walk as Christians? How does one walk by faith, and what character qualities would be required to do so (trust, obedience, etc.)? How could you apply this verse in a situation that was completely unexpected and perhaps unwelcome in your life?

Read: 2 Timothy 4:1-2

Reflect:

In whose name does Paul charge us to be ready? When are we to be ready? In season and out means day or night (the night before the conference in my case), whether you're tired or not, weekend or weekday. What are we to be prepared to do? What does this tell you about flexibility and obedience?

Read: Luke 12:35-38

Reflect:

In this passage, Jesus is speaking of the end times, telling us to be ready for his unexpected return. How does this apply to being flexible? Do you think in your own life that God would find you ready and waiting were he to come today? Why or why not?

Journey Journal

Journey IV

Ruth:
A Young Woman of Faithfulness

Your people shall be my people,
and your God my God.

Chapter 10
Journey of Faith

The world is perfect today. The sun is sparkling on the fields of grain and the wind is blowing softly through the trees. All of nature is praising God today, just as I do. I am so thankful for the beauty, and for this home, they are blessings from God.

My journey here, both physically and spiritually, has been a long and hard one. Sometimes I thought it would be impossible to take another step, sometimes I felt as if God were asking the impossible of me. But every step has led me closer to knowing him and closer to peace.

My story is one of hardship and pain, grief and joy, faithfulness, and a trust unshaken in God. It is a story of God's leading and my following. It begs to be told, and I hope that somehow it will touch your heart. This journey has changed me forever.

My story begins in Moab, a nation of idols and revelry, among a race of people dedicated to the worship of Baal and Chemosh, two pagan gods. My parents, like the rest of the culture, were faithful worshippers of the idols. They raised me to be just like them, and as far back as I can remember I took part with them in the worship and rituals, cringing at the unspeakable horror of the ceremonies.

From my earliest childhood, I could never fully understand the idols. I prayed with the others, but I never saw or felt anything that could shake my conviction, hidden deep in my heart, that they were but pieces of wood and stone. But I never told anyone my doubts, I was afraid of what they might do to me, for the people were dedicated to the idols, and the priests were evil.

I longed for something—I didn't know what. But I knew that somehow the idol worship wasn't right, that those gods were powerless, and that the rituals and worship surrounding them were evil.

Surely there was more. Surely, the idols weren't the real gods, could such gods create a beautiful world? But I was a timid girl. I never asked any questions about the idols or did anything that would separate me from the others in my culture. I couldn't stand the thought of being rejected.

As I grew older, the emptiness in my heart grew greater and greater; there was a longing in my heart that was never satisfied. When I reached the age where I was to marry, I despaired. The mere thought of giving myself to one of the boys I knew, all drunk, loud and rash, made me cringe. But every respectable girl in our circle of friends did, and according to my father, marry I would.

One evening, after a long, loud argument with my parents about my hesitation to choose a husband, I escaped into the cool air outside and walked down to the grove of trees at the edge of the city. As I stood still in the twilight, I jumped, as out of the corner of my eye I saw a man get up. I had thought I was alone.

Turning around, I saw Mahlon, the son of a respected Jewish family with whom my father did business. He sat silently under a tree, facing toward the setting sun, his head bowed in prayer. I marveled at the freedom he felt to pray to his God in any place.

I was watching him so intently that when he suddenly turned to go, I jumped. After a polite greeting, he left me, but I sat for awhile longer in the orchard, for my mind had been opened to the possibility of other gods, and surely Mahlon's god must be gentle, to allow such casual prayer.

After that, I began to notice the times when Mahlon's father would come to our house. Often Mahlon was with him, and I would manage to speak with him for a few minutes before he left. Through these quick snatches of conversation, I began to know Mahlon. He was so different from the other boys I knew: where they were loud and shallow, he was quiet, polite and thoughtful.

One day, on a warm afternoon when Mahlon had come to our house with his father, I took him out to the garden, and asked him the question that had been in my heart for quite some time.

"Mahlon," I began, feeling awkward, "what is it that makes you different, I mean in a good way! You are good, and gentle, so unlike the other men I know. What is it?"

"Oh Ruth," he said, turning to me with a sparkle of excitement in his eyes, "it is Jehovah, my God, and oh Ruth, he is loving, powerful, the only true God. I have wanted so much to tell you about him Ruth, He is merciful, and gentle, and he is faithful, doing only what is best for his people."

I was astonished—one god? Could there really be only one god? I had been raised believing in many gods, and none of them were loving, or merciful. It was almost too wonderful to be true.

Mahlon's answer was the beginning of many intense hours of discussion, hours that brought about a change in my heart. Through Mahlon I learned of God and his love. I learned of my own sin. And for the first time, I found a love that would fill every longing of my heart.

But deep down I was still fearful. I could not find the courage to tell my parents of my newfound faith. What if they threw me out of the house? What if all my friends rejected me? What if my whole life became uncertain?

Over time, Mahlon and I fell in love. How could we help it? And it was the best kind of love, a love born out of a search for God, and I loved Mahlon all the more for leading me to the God I had embraced. When Mahlon asked my father for permission to marry me, my father said a hearty yes, for Mahlon came from a well-respected family. The fact that they were foreign seemed not to matter.

When we were married and happily settled in our new home, I felt for the first time in my life that I had come into happiness. Mahlon was faithful and loving. His mother Naomi, a widow, devoted herself to me, and our home flourished. The only thorn in my happiness was the fact that my parents did not share my faith. But I had found that the anger I had so feared from my parents over my religion was not an issue, for as Mahlon's wife I was expected to adopt his beliefs. So, I was completely satisfied; God had blessed me and I was at peace with the world.

And then it happened. Even after many years, I still sometimes feel the shock of it. Mahlon died. He was well and healthy one day and dead the next, struck down in the night by a raging fever that swept our city. I was so numb I couldn't even cry. How could God do this to me? We had been so happy, it had never occurred to me that it could all be taken away. But it was, and I was left in complete desolation.

When I found out that Naomi had decided to journey back to her own land, I felt as if there was nothing left for me to do but die. I can still remember the emptiness in my heart as I felt everything I loved being torn from me. My only option was to return to the house of my parents, but the thought completely crushed me.

Knowing God as I knew him by then, I couldn't possibly take part in my culture's idol worship again. To be trapped in that emptiness would be unbearable. Though my parents accepted my faith when I was married, they would expect me to once again return to the idol worship when I came back to their home as a widow. The thought of my father's anger at my refusal was enough to make me tremble. Besides that, my father would make every effort to remarry me to one to one of the drunken, rich men I so loathed.

I can still remember the dark day in my painfully silent house when I grew quiet enough to feel God come near—and then my tears came. For hours I cried and raged against the pain and unfairness of my lot. When I was finally quiet, God began to speak. What was I to do? I asked. And within my heart, I heard both an answer and a question. "Go with Naomi. Stay with your new family, the family I have given you. But you must trust me. Are you willing, Ruth? Can you release your fears to me?"

Could I? I had always, since childhood, been fearful at heart: I had feared my parents and the idols and other people's opinions. When Mahlon led me to God, I lost my fear of the idols, but my underlying fear of man was still there.

And did I trust God? Could I? Of course I worshipped him, but I had always depended on Mahlon. I hadn't needed to depend on God—Mahlon had always been there for me. But now, with everything I had always depended on taken away, I saw that without God, I was helpless. Now, I had to make my decision, I had to trust God, or be doomed to fear and despair for the rest of my life.

Finally, after hours of tears and desperate prayers, I made my decision, and went the very next day to tell my father that I was accompanying Naomi to Bethlehem.

I can still remember the day when I walked into his business room. I cringed, for the cold hard walls and emotionless decorations of statues and idols reminded me of my father's stubbornness. When he turned toward me, I began quickly, resolved to get everything out before I lost my courage.

"Father," I began, my voice seeming to fade into a whisper against those walls, "I have come to tell you of my decision in regard to my future. I am returning to Israel with Naomi."

For a moment I waited, trying to see what his reaction would be, but there was nothing but a steely glint in his hard eyes.

"Father, I love you and mother, so very much, and I thank you for all you have done for me," I began, trying to soften my words, "but I feel called by God to go to Bethlehem, and I am resolved."

It was just as I expected, my father's face grew red with rage, and I felt myself quiver like I always had when my father's violent anger was unleashed against me. I could feel my whole body tensing as he stomped toward me, and began shouting, cursing the day such a disobedient daughter was born. For a moment, I was numb, and I was afraid the fear of my father would once again overwhelm me, but suddenly in the midst of that storm, I remembered something Mahlon had said.

"Our God is powerful Ruth, and he will always help us."

In that instant I knew. I knew. My father, my friends, my family, no longer had control over me. God was the one with the power, and I never had to fear anyone or anything again. God was greater than everything else, and I placed my trust completely in him.

And so I began my journey of faith. It was a bumpy start, but a start nonetheless. All that remained now was to tell Naomi of my decision. Casting my lot with her would be a step into a future, a land and a life I knew nothing of. But I knew what God had told me, I knew that he would go with me. With God as my guide, how could I be afraid?

"No! I will not leave you! Please, please let me come with you."

Ruth knelt at Naomi's feet, weeping as if her heart would break. Silent, the older woman searched the desert landscape with her eyes. Much more of this pleading and her barrier of resistance would break down. She did love Ruth, terribly, but no—she would not ruin the girl's life just to meet her own needs. She couldn't allow her son's widow to return with her to her Jewish homeland, where she would be a foreigner, alone and friendless except for Naomi, who was herself a widow.

Naomi knew what it was like to be alone and friendless, a widow adrift in a foreign land, feeling as if God himself had forsaken her. It was miserable. She could not let Ruth do it. Orpah, Ruth's sister-in-law, had already left Naomi, seeing the impossibility of the journey to a new land.

Naomi knew, too, that Ruth was fearful by nature, unsuited for the new life she would have to lead in Israel. She would never forgive herself if the timid girl should break under the pressures she would face. Kneeling down and cradling Ruth's face in her hands, she spoke softly, as if talking to a stubborn child.

"Ruth, I love you, but you must return to your parents' home. Orpah has already left, and you must go as well. Go back with her to your own people. I am old and soon will die, and you would be left all alone. You are a Moabitess. Go home."

Looking down at Ruth, Naomi saw the same love-hungry pleading in her eyes that had first made Naomi love her so much. It tore at her heart, but she must keep strong in her resolve!

Ruth bowed her head for a moment. When she raised her eyes again, they held a light Naomi had never seen before, and when she spoke, her voice was as strong and determined as Naomi had ever heard it. "You are wrong, Naomi. I am no longer a Moabitess. For where you go, I will go, and where you lodge, there I will be. Your people shall be my people, and your God shall be my God. Where you die, I will die, and there I will be buried. Thus may the Lord do to me, and worse, if anything but death parts you and me."

The words hung in the air between them. Naomi stared at Ruth, seeing within her a resolve and confidence she had never seen before. Her daughter-in-law had always been a timid girl, but there was nothing timid about her now. A great change had come over her. Naomi could see in her eyes the same dedication and purpose that Naomi herself had felt so many years ago, before bitterness had driven all joy from her heart.

And Ruth had sworn by the Lord God, a solemn thing indeed, she reminded herself. Her vow was clearly heartfelt.

A sudden sense of God's presence rose up in Naomi's heart, a feeling that had not been there for a long time. With it came a different answer to Ruth's plea:

"Yes. Yes, Ruth! Come with me! And may God go with us both, for we'll surely need him!"

Not an hour later, arm in arm, Ruth and Naomi began their journey—a journey of faith to a new land, a new home and a new life, and neither of them looked back.

This story is taken from Ruth 1

Reflections

Cold and tired, the young woman stepped off the train and looked around at the new city that would be her home. A gray sky and dirty streets met the young woman's eyes, and an air of depression hung over everything. Even after thirty years, Warsaw, Poland was still recovering from the devastation of WWII, and she could see that there was much work to be done. It was the reason she had come.

The young woman who got off the train in Warsaw that day was my mother. She had taken a step of faith, leaving her stable life in America to be a missionary to Communist Poland. She had no idea what she was getting into; all she knew was that God had called her, and where he called she would follow.

My mom has told us many stories about her three years in Poland, when the country was still behind the Iron Curtain. Believe me, she has many fascinating stories to tell. But what has always amazed me the most is that she went there in the first place.

She's told us of the night she sat in a huge auditorium with hundreds of other committed Christians, listening to a missionary tell of the need for workers in Poland. It was as if God reached down and touched her heart, she says, as if he asked her right then to go to Poland. Within a few months she had done just that. She stepped out in faith and moved to a foreign country with only love for the Lord to keep her going.

Taking a step of faith like my mother did is harder than it sounds. I'm sure she had doubts about her decision. I know that her friends and family urged her to stay, and she must have been afraid of what might happen if she was caught by the secret police. But she went anyway.

Ruth was like that. Can you imagine? She was a widow, still grieving her husband, feeling utterly alone, and she heard God tell her to move to a foreign country where Moabites were often ostracized. She must have wondered what to do. She would be so alone. Naomi was devoted, but bitter, and she wouldn't always be there, and there were so many fears and hurdles to overcome. But in the end, Ruth took that amazing step of faith, and it led her to blessings she could never have imagined.

We are so comfortable in our modern world, and so unwilling to step out of our comfort zones. But following God takes faith and often involves stepping into the completely unknown. We need to be more like Ruth, who had her fears but ultimately overcame them with faith.

One day as I thought about my spiritual heroes, I wondered in my heart how I, too, could take a step of faith like the ones they had taken. I was only seventeen, still a student, so I couldn't move to Poland quite yet.

What I realized that day was that taking a step of faith doesn't always mean moving to a different country. As I am a bit shy and self-conscious, a step of faith for me might be telling my unbelieving neighbor about the Lord. Taking a risk like that—stepping into an area where I don't know what will happen, having to trust that God will work everything together for good—requires faith.

Taking a step of faith can be reaching out to an unlovable person who might reject me. Taking a step of faith can be reaching out to the lonely person in a group. Taking a step of faith can be going on a mission trip. Many areas in my life require faith. When I hear God's voice, I need to listen—and follow.

As I get older and so many choices lie before me, I want to remember Ruth and my mom and so many others who provide a role model for me, so that I, too, can learn to follow God. Someday, maybe I, too, can take the big step of faith that will change my life forever. When the opportunity comes, I want to be ready.

Read: Hebrews 11:1

Reflect:
What is faith? What do you think the writer means when he talks about "things not seen"? What do you think the unseen things were in Ruth's life? How about your own?

Read: John 14:12

Reflect:
What does this verse say that anyone who has faith can do? What kind of faith or foundation of belief do you have to have in order to perform miracles? Do you think that sometimes God is just waiting for us to have enough faith to work miracles?

Read: Matthew 9:27-29

Reflect:

Why were the blind men healed? Why do you think faith was so important to Jesus? Do you think you can really follow him without faith?

Read: Hebrews 10:38

Reflect:

Who is to live by faith? What will happen if we shrink back from following God? Why do you think the righteous have to live by faith? Is there an area in your life in which you need to have faith?

Journey IV   *Ruth*

Journey Journal

Chapter 11
Heart of Diligence

"There's a lot of work to be done, that's for sure," Naomi remarked in her matter-of-fact way. *We had reached our new home, and it stood before us in the blazing sunshine of the morning, old, abandoned and in all other ways looking very forlorn. I gazed up at the dark windows and sagging ceiling and then turned my eyes to the overgrown garden and broken fence. I felt like crying. This was my new home?*

Walking up to the front step, I dropped my bag beside me and sat down just for a moment as my shoulders sagged with weariness. I was exhausted. We had just finished the long journey from Moab to Bethlehem, and the hot days of endless walking under the blistering sun were taking their toll on my strength.

The strength in my heart was waning, too. Feeling the sort of despair that always comes when a person is physically worn out, I felt discouraged and doubtful. Had I done the right thing?

I had tried to be strong in the past weeks, but I felt my energy dissipating. With a dull ache hidden beneath my resolve of happiness, I missed Mahlon. The pain of my grief brought up so many questions: Would I be even more alone among the people of Bethlehem than in Moab? Was I right to leave everything I had known up to a short time ago? I was a foreigner in this land, and a foreign widow at that. What would

I do when Naomi was gone?

I sat on the steps, a thousand doubts and questions filling my mind. But just as the tears threatened to come, I thought of Naomi's words and stood up. There was work to be done, and God had called me to do it. I needed to stop worrying, and instead, walk resolutely ahead into the new life I knew in my heart God had called me to. If I could just push away the dark thoughts for the moment and get to work, I knew I would feel better—especially after we set everything to right.

Turning to Naomi, I managed a smile. I opened the door into the old house. A dusty, mildewed smell reached me, and I could barely see ahead for the shadows and cobwebs. But despite all of that, I could see the room was large, and once fixed up would be inviting and cheerful.

Within hours of our arrival, we were deep into our work. Though we were tired, we were eager to get the house livable again. Our bags, blankets, and few precious belongings lay spread out on the floor, and we cleaned and scrubbed, trying to revive the old house into a home. By nightfall, we had made great progress. I went to sleep exhausted but happier.

That was the first day in a long line of workdays as Naomi and I struggled to bring the house and land back to their former wholeness, as well as provide food for us. I'll never forget those first weeks in my new home. I explored the fields and roads between working, and I began to meet some of the Jewish people, though few were overly friendly.

It was a time of learning for me. Learning to work, learning to trust God, and learning to walk in joy. The sun shone brightly every day, and I woke each morning to the sound of the wind in the fields instead of the shouts of people. I felt so blessed to be able to worship the Lord freely, and though I was unable to go to the Sabbath meetings because I was a Moabite, I was able now to worship God as I pleased. I could do that just as well in a windswept field as in a building.

I had my unhappy moments, but I was learning to work through them and keep going. Walking through the fields and forests always helped me.

Naomi had met up with her old friends again, and it nearly broke my heart when I heard her tell them to call her Mara, "the bitter one," instead of Naomi. I began to see Naomi as a challenge; I wanted, if at all possible, to bring joy back to her heart.

I think the villagers were shocked upon seeing me at first, I looked different from them in my dress and even my hair, and I overheard whispers of amazement that Naomi had brought me back with her. But eventually they grew used to me, and when they came to visit Naomi, didn't stare as they had at first.

When we had been in Bethlehem almost a month, I saw that our supply of food was running out, and I knew that I needed to find a new source of grain for our bread besides what we already had stored, most of it the gifts of kind neighbors.

I wasn't too worried, for I knew of the Hebrew law allowing widows and the very poor to glean in the fields of landowners. I had already picked the field where I could gather grain left behind by the harvesters. I saw that many women gleaned there, which caused me to think that the owner might be more generous than some of the others. As a foreigner, I would perhaps not be as welcome in some fields.

On the morning of my first day to glean, I got up early and prayed, thanking God with all my heart for the new life he had given me. When I rose from my knees that morning, I was sure that the day held blessing. Eager to see what awaited me in the golden fields and to find out yet another aspect of the new land where I lived, I started out.

Pale and golden, the sunshine streamed through the clouds and lit the long fields of grain below with summer brightness. Boaz, a respected and wealthy man in the Bethlehem community, looked over the rolling countryside, feeling satisfied and content. It was harvest time, and as he leisurely rode through the fields, his men called out greetings to him on all sides. He felt that God had blessed him greatly. He had worked many years, and God had fulfilled his dreams of a prosperous business and a comfortable home.

When he reached the small tents set up along the edge of the fields as resting and meal shelters, he dismounted and strode up to his overseer, who was tallying the amounts of the grain collected in the past days.

"Good morning, Jacob," he called out heartily.

"Good morning, Master Boaz," replied the overseer pleasantly. "I've just been counting the bundles of grain. We've done quite well the past few days, even better than last year's crop."

Smiling, Boaz gazed over the field of harvesters and gleaners.

"Those are hardworking men, Jacob. And those women, they're hardworking, too. Are the men leaving enough grain for them? I don't want the men to be careless, but it wouldn't hurt to leave enough for the women to fill their sacks. I know they need it."

With a smile, Jacob turned to Boaz. "Master, you are certainly a generous man. It's a pity you have no wife and children to share your kind heart."

Boaz thanked his overseer with one of his well-known smiles, then turned his eyes to the place where a group of women were working. "Jacob, who is that woman? There, see? The one with the basket and the red scarf."

Looking out over the women, Jacob spotted the one Boaz had pointed to.

"Why, that is the Moabitess who came back with Naomi. Surely you have heard of Naomi's return to Bethlehem. The girl asked me this morning if she could glean in our fields, and I told her yes, of course. She has been working hard ever since, with only a short break. She was very gracious," he added, "and she's a diligent girl—even if she is a foreigner."

Boaz was greatly interested in Naomi and her daughter-in-law. With a thoughtful gaze, Boaz watched as Ruth kept diligently at her work, stopping to help an older woman with her basket. He had heard of Ruth. In fact, Naomi was a distant relation to him through her husband, and he had been both happy and surprised when he heard of her return. He was especially surprised when he heard of the Moabitess she had brought with her, and that the girl feared the one true God.

As of yet, he hadn't visited the women, but he had been very curious about them, feeling both pity for Naomi and interest in the young girl who had come so far from her homeland. It pleased Boaz, and made him all the more interested to meet Ruth, when he heard the townspeople talk admiringly of her. To hear the people in town, who were always suspicious of foreigners, speak highly of the integrity of Ruth was testimony to her character.

He watched as Ruth dropped behind the group, dropping her bundle for a moment of rest. She stood alone, and acting on impulse, Boaz began to walk toward her. Finally he would meet this interesting young woman.

Ruth was tired from the heat of the day but satisfied with her work; her grain sack was growing heavy. The task was exhausting, but she was beginning to get used to it.

She straightened for a moment to ease the ache in her back, shading her eyes as she turned her gaze to the far end of the field where tents were set up for thirsty workers. But she was startled to see a tall man coming toward her, and with a start she realized it was the owner of the field coming to speak with her. She had seen him ride up on his horse, and she had watched his greetings to the workers. Why would he want to talk to her?

Worried, she wondered anxiously if he was coming to tell her she couldn't glean in his fields. Though she had not found trouble thus far, she knew that foreigners weren't always welcomed.

She couldn't have been more surprised when, as Boaz came near, he called out, "My daughter, hello!" Ruth watched him approach, too astonished to know what to do. As he came near, she bowed her head slightly out of respect, and not knowing what to say, waited for him to speak.

"Please listen to me," he said. "Don't go and glean in anyone else's field—stay here with my servant girls. Watch where the men are harvesting, and follow the other women. They seem to always know where the best grain is."

Here he stopped, and Ruth dared to meet his eyes. She smiled shyly but gratefully at the amazing kindness he was showing her, and he smiled back with a smile she liked very much.

"I have told my men not to touch you—you need not fear for your safety," he said. "And whenever you are thirsty, please, feel free to get a drink from the jars of water my men have filled."

Ruth stared at him in amazement. Bowing low to the ground in the manner of the country, she thanked him for his kindness and then asked a question: "Why have I found such favor in your eyes, that you would even notice me? I'm a foreigner!"

Ruth watched closely as Boaz smiled at her.

"I've been told of all that you've done for your mother-in-law since the death of your husband," he said, "leaving everything you'd ever known, your family and homeland, to come to live among us, in a country you had never even seen."

Reaching out, Boaz placed his hand on Ruth's shoulder, and held her eyes with a serious gaze.

"May the Lord repay you for what you have done, and may you be richly rewarded by the Lord, the God of Israel, under whose wings you have taken refuge."

Ruth smiled up at him, a warm, grateful smile. He was one of the first people to really encourage her, care about her since she had made her journey, and she was so thankful.

"Thank you," she said sincerely. "I hope I will continue to please you. You have given me comfort." Her eyes grew misty. "You have spoken so kindly to me, even though I don't have the standing even of one of your servant girls."

With a final smile at her words, Boaz walked away, leaving Ruth to look after him in amazement.

Boaz was well pleased with his encounter with Ruth, and as he worked that morning, his thoughts were still on the gracious young woman in the field.

He had been greatly impressed by her humility and goodness, and as he continued to watch her, he saw firsthand how faithful she was. He supposed it was her faithfulness that had really interested him in the first place. He had heard glowing reports of her work around the house, the gathering of her grain, her worship of the Lord. Yes, Ruth was a faithful woman, as well as gracious and beautiful, and that was something Boaz greatly admired.

"Naomi," I called, running into our home, "Naomi! I have such wonderful news! Are you here?"

Coming in through the side door, Naomi smiled a greeting and eagerly began to question me.

"Where did you glean today? Do you know the name of the lord of the field?"

She stopped suddenly as she saw my full bags. She knew that I could not have gleaned that much unless the owner himself had been kind to me.

"Why, who was it, Ruth? May God bless him!"

"His name is Boaz," I began excitedly.

Naomi interrupted me with her exclamation: "The Lord be praised! Boaz has not stopped showing kindness to the living or the dead! Ruth, he is one of our relatives! He is a kinsman redeemer—if we ever are in great need, he will help us!"

"Why, I can't believe it, Naomi! He even had me share his lunch, and he told me to stay in his fields until the end of the harvest."

"Oh yes, yes, you must, Ruth," said Naomi, her eyes glowing. "It will be so good, because elsewhere you might have been harmed. Oh Ruth, God is finally bringing blessing back. He has been so good to us."

I couldn't have agreed more. As I lay down to sleep that night, I thanked God for his blessings once again. I was so happy, and I greatly admired Boaz. He had the same kind ease that had first attracted me to Mahlon. Truly, he was a righteous man. The next day I returned to his fields, and every day after that until the harvest was over.

So a new season in my life began. A time of work, a time to cultivate faithfulness. I tried to follow to the best of my ability the road set before me. And I found joy along the way.

Every day I worked in the fields, gathering food. Every day I worked around our house. And every day I worked on Naomi's heart. The days passed pleasantly, my routine brightened occasionally by kind words from Boaz. I was learning so much as I watched God faithfully provide for us. I saw his faithfulness in every part of my life, and I was faithful to obey him, too.

Amidst the routine of my days, I saw his beauty. I learned what it meant to be fulfilled in his joy. I learned to enjoy hard work. And yes, I learned to love my new home, a place that offered me warmth and security. I felt, too, that my heart had come to a new place. The longings I had so often felt began to subside.

I began to feel, after many years of wandering in a spiritual desert, that my heart had finally come home.

This story is taken from Ruth 2

Reflections

"He who is faithful in small things will be faithful also in much…"

I was sick of those words! How many times would Mom repeat them to me? There is a limit to how faithful one can be, and I felt that I had definitely reached that limit. Storming to my room, I shut the door as hard as I dared and fell in a lump of frustration and tears on the bed.

I was so tired of having to do so many mundane, faithful things. Even more, I was tired of Mom telling me that those mundane things would be the making of my character! How would doing obscure math problems make me great?

My tantrum was the climax of a rather awful week, and I was as discouraged as I could be. Every day had been more of a downer than the day before. Between little disturbances with my brothers, petty arguments with friends and lots of housework for the holidays, I was about to burst. Actually, I had burst; I finally lost my patience and temper when one of the boys teased me.

When Mom corrected me for my bad attitude, I felt as if the whole world was unfair, and when she gently reminded me of our verse of the month, I felt that I couldn't take any more. I'd been faithful long enough! In fact, I felt that all the dreary duties and tasks I was expected to do were taking all my time, dragging me down—and I wondered if anything I was doing really mattered. Faithfulness didn't seem to be getting me anywhere.

Once in my room, I sat down on my bed, where my Bible was sitting open invitingly. But in a contrary mood I turned instead to another book I'd been reading, *At the Back of the North Wind*—the story of a small boy who travels to the back of the north wind (heaven), learns the song of heaven and carries it in his heart back to earth. With the image of heaven in his heart, his mission is to bring its peace to those around him. As I began to read, my eyes fell on these words:

> *Diamond's father and mother were rather miserable, and Diamond began to feel a kind of darkness beginning to spread over his own mind. But the same moment he said to himself, "This will never do. I can't give in to this. I've been to the back of the north wind. Things go right there, so I must try to get things to go right here. I've got to fight the miserable things. They shan't make me miserable if I can help it."*

Leaning back and letting the book fall on my lap, I realized that I wanted to be like Diamond, fighting the miserable things and being faithful in the everyday things of life. I had failed that day to remember that whatever I do, I am serving God. As I read that passage, I saw that I still needed to be faithful. Perhaps through my work in the little things, I, too, could fight the misery.

When I finally opened my Bible, I went to the book of Ruth. There I saw faithfulness in action. Ruth must have wondered what purpose God had for her in her new land. She had taken a step of faith and made the long journey, but she had to wonder why God had led her there. Was she simply going to care for Naomi, clean and make meals for the rest of her life?

Despite the questions she must have had, Ruth kept on faithfully. She worked on the house, making it once again into a home. She faithfully cared for Naomi, gathered grain every day for their meals and built a reputation of godliness in the village. She was faithful in every aspect of her life.

Sometimes God asks me to serve him in the mundane. He wants me to be willing to be faithful in every job he brings my way, not just the exciting ones: "He who is faithful in small things will be faithful also in much." My faithfulness to little things does make up my character. My attitude about them can please God or bring him sorrow, and unless I learn to be faithful in the small things, God can never trust me to be faithful in the big things of life.

Now, when I feel frustration coming over me, I try to think of Diamond and Ruth and all the others who have been faithful in small things, and I remind myself that God is watching for me to be faithful as well.

So whenever you find yourself called to serve in the little things, take a few moments to go outside, look up into the sky and thank God for his love. Remember that your small acts of faithfulness count in a big way. And then go back inside to finish one more lesson, clean up one more thing or say one more kind word—knowing that just like Diamond, you are bringing a little bit of heaven to the world by being faithful.

Read: Galatians 6:9

Reflect:

What are we not to grow weary of? What will happen if we don't give up? What is something in your life in which you can actively keep on doing good? What will your harvest be?

Read: Romans 12:11

Reflect:

What are we not to lack? What is our spirit to be like? What is the goal of our zeal? What are some words that would describe a zealous person for the Lord? Do these words apply to you?

Read: Matthew 9:37-38

Reflect:

For what does Jesus say we should pray? Why do you think the workers are few? Do you think some people give up when the work gets hard or tedious? How can you be one of the harvesters? Are you willing to keep working in the small parts of the harvest as well as the big?

Read: Matthew 25:14-30

Reflect:

This passage is a parable of the kingdom of heaven. Why do you think the wicked servant buried his talent in the ground? What does the master call the servants who did well? What was their reward? How do you think this applies to the little things in life?

Journey IV   *Ruth*

Journey Journal

Chapter 12
The Great Reward

Warm and golden, the late afternoon sun shone happily down on the harvested fields, lighting up the hidden paths and homes around them and brightening the road as Ruth made her way home. With a contented sigh, she shifted a heavy bag of grain from one arm to another as she walked along the dirt path. The day had been good, full of harvesting the last of the grain and finishing the last bit of work around the house.

Still, a sense of sadness hung over her heart. The summer harvest had been so fulfilling, full of golden days in the fields, plenty of food, and time spent with Boaz, whom Ruth was learning to respect and admire more every day. He had started to visit their little home from time-to-time always bringing a gift of food or a small household item, and Ruth looked forward to his visits with great anticipation. But soon, the harvest would come to an end, and Ruth knew that Boaz would be wrapped up in his business. She already felt a sense of loneliness

As she passed through the small fence that led to the home she shared with Naomi, Ruth looked around her at the tall shade trees, the newly scrubbed house, the garden with its even rows of vegetables, and she felt proud. She had worked hard all summer to bring life to the old house, and now it seemed that everything was finally running smoothly.

But deep in her heart, Ruth was lonely. She wondered sometimes what her future held. Would she ever remarry? Would there ever be more to her life than the day-to-day work she performed? She didn't know, and she felt helpless to do anything about it. Would anything ever come of her faithfulness?

Sometimes she prayed that God would give her a family again—a husband to love and protect her, children to guide and love, and home for all of them to share. The prospect made her sigh with delight.

If the truth were told, deep in her heart she admired Boaz as much as any other man she had ever met. She loved his smile, his integrity, his goodness and kindness. But she was a foreigner and so far beneath him. It was pure folly to dwell on Boaz, so she tried not to.

The warm, inviting aroma of freshly baked bread greeted her as she climbed the three stone steps to the house. She eagerly set down her bag of grain and walked to the open fire, soaking in the warmth and the delicious smell of the bread.

"Hello, Ruth," came Naomi's kind voice from a chair in the shadowy corner. "Did your day go well, my dear?"

With a smile, Ruth turned to Naomi.

"Oh yes, it went very well, and I have yet more grain. Boaz was, as always, very kind."

"Yes," said Naomi quietly—and rather strangely, Ruth thought. "I'm sure he was."

Throughout the rest of the afternoon and evening, Ruth noticed an air of thoughtfulness that hovered over Naomi, and several times she almost asked if something was troubling her, but decided against it. Naomi would tell her when and if she wanted to.

Later that night, after all the bustle of the evening meal was over, the two women sat down by the dying fire for a few moments of warmth before bed, and Naomi finally told Ruth what was on her mind.

"Ruth, my child," Naomi began softly, reaching over to take Ruth's hand, "You have been my help and comfort, and I thank God every day for you. But you are young. A woman your age should have friends and family, and pleasant things to do. Should I not try to find a home for you where you would be well provided for?"

Ruth began to protest that she was happy, and already well provided for, but Naomi's lifted eyebrows silenced her.

"No, Ruth, a vibrant young woman like you needs a husband and family. You have so much to give. My child, as you know, Boaz is our kinsman, and he is a good man." Here Naomi paused. Her expression was serious. "Ruth, I want Boaz to marry you. As a near kinsman, it is his duty. And—" She smiled. "I don't think he will find it a chore."

Ruth blushed. Naomi had seen right through her. And could it be, as she implied, that Boaz looked on her with more than friendship?

"Ruth, listen to me." Naomi cupped Ruth's face in her hands and looked at her intently. "Boaz will be threshing wheat tonight and staying out in his fields. Here is what you must do: Go wash and dress yourself; make yourself beautiful and perfume yourself. Then go down to Boaz. Wait until he has finished eating and drinking and has gone to lie down. Then go over, uncover his feet, and wait for him to respond. He will understand and will tell you what to do."

Ruth stared at Naomi, her eyes wide and her brow furrowed.

"You must trust me," Naomi said, a new note of confidence and command in her voice. "I have thought of this for many days. Do what I have said."

Ruth nodded. "Yes, Naomi. It will be done as you have said."

I felt in shock as I left to go to my room. That my life might change so suddenly was both exciting and confusing. Perhaps it was what I had prayed for, but I still felt numb as I went about my preparations.

I knew of the Jewish law providing for a widow to be protected by marriage to a near kinsman, but I wondered if the law applied to me. Would Boaz reject me because I was foreign? In my own eyes I was unworthy of him.

I had never heard of a woman doing this to get a husband before, and I almost laughed at the situation. God was most certainly involved in this, and it seemed to me he must have a sense of humor.

I understood why I must go at night; there might be scandal or gossip if I approached Boaz during the day, and he was rarely alone anyway. Yet it seemed such a bold thing to do.

Nonetheless, I obeyed, trusting that Naomi and God knew what they were doing. With furtive, quiet steps, I made my way across the fields, the moonlight showing me the way. My lips moved silently in prayer as my feet bent the flattened grain stalks. I just hoped God would bless Naomi's plan—and my obedience.

I knew I was near Boaz' fields when I saw the firelight by which the last workers were eating their supper. Quietly I slipped behind some grain bales where I could wait for Boaz to be alone.

It all happened just as Naomi had said. Soon the men left and Boaz lay down on a small pallet to guard his harvest. With a furiously beating heart, I made my way to his feet and uncovered them, which awakened him. He looked about, and seeing me in the darkness, started violently. "Who is it?" he asked, his whisper loud.

Trembling all over, I knelt before him.

"Please, Boaz, agree to protect me, for you are my kinsman redeemer, the only relative of my dead husband."

"The Lord bless you, my daughter," he replied, standing up in the darkness, and a deep sigh of relief ran through me. "You have shown great kindness to me by coming to me for help instead of going after a younger man."

At this rather surprising statement, I glanced up. Boaz was so far above me, and he was one of the only men who would consider me as a wife, since I was a foreigner. I admired him above all others. I felt greatly blessed.

"Don't be afraid, my daughter," Boaz continued, kneeling down to look at me, the moon on his face. "I will do for you all that you ask. Everyone in the village knows you are a woman of noble character."

Here, however, he stopped, and I saw his eyebrows furrow.

"Ruth, though I am near of kin, there is another nearer than I."

I felt all my hopes suddenly fall. Who was this other man? Was he a man as kind and good as Boaz? If he wanted to take me as his wife and buy Naomi's land to protect the two of us, I would be bound to him.

Boaz knelt beside me and placed his hand on my shoulder.

"Ruth, if he agrees to be the kinsman redeemer to you, I must step aside. But if he doesn't...." Boaz looked deeply into my eyes. "With the Lord as my witness, I will do everything you ask. Now, stay here until morning. I would not have you hurt going back through the fields in the night."

So I found a place to rest until morning, and then, when the first rays of the sun turned the sky a soft blue, I crept away and walked slowly home.

As the horizon slowly began to glow pink, I stopped to sit under an old tree to collect my thoughts. My heart and mind were all in a flurry. I could barely comprehend what was happening. Yesterday I had longed for a home and wondered if Boaz could ever love me. This morning, a whole new life was before me. But what kind of life? What was going to happen? I tried to pray, but I felt once more as if I was walking ahead into darkness.

Would I ever be free and at rest again? I didn't know—but still, I obeyed. There was nothing else to do.

With an impatient look toward the road, Boaz crossed his arms and began to pace back and forth under the tent with anxious footsteps. Where was Japheth? Every morning he came into the town square to speak with the elders and other men, and this day, Boaz had a very important issue to discuss with him. But the man was dreadfully late.

Boaz glanced back into the tent at Ruth, who was sitting in the corner, appearing very calm, and gave her a reassuring smile. But he was nervous. As the nearer kinsman, Japheth had first rights to buy Naomi's land and to offer himself as the two widows' protector, and while Boaz knew he was an honest and hardworking man, he could also be cold and harsh at times. But aside from that, Boaz had realized early that morning as he watched Ruth leave for home through the fields that he truly did love her.

He respected her for her integrity and faithfulness, loved her for her sweet and gentle spirit and rejoiced that she worshipped the same God as he. Surely God would bring them together. For years Boaz had longed for a wife and family, but God had never blessed him in that way. Now, the door seemed to be opening, and Boaz sensed in his heart that God had saved Ruth just for him.

Turning around again, Boaz hurried out to the road as he saw the familiar figure of Japheth strolling into the village.

"Japheth!" he called, and drew him into the small tent where the elders of the town kept their counsel. In short order, he laid out the situation before Japheth. "If you cannot or do not wish to fulfill this duty," he concluded, "I am next in line and will do this thing for Naomi and her daughter-in-law Ruth."

He watched Japheth uneasily as a greedy smile lit the man's face. Land was a precious possession, and no man would pass up a chance to acquire more.

Boaz stepped forward and looked him straight in the eye. "I must remind you, Japheth, that if you buy the land, you will also acquire Ruth as your wife." Watching Japheth carefully, he held out his arm to Ruth, who rose from her seat and came demurely forward, her head bowed.

Japheth grew suddenly agitated. Boaz knew exactly what he was thinking. Marry Ruth? A foreigner? Besides, his wife would be very angry. He didn't want another wife!

He cleared his throat. "Boaz, I cannot redeem this land and marry this woman," he said. "It would endanger my own property. You take her and buy the land yourself."

Boaz was overjoyed, and there in the sight of all the elders of the town, the deal was made. Japheth formally refused to buy the land, Boaz accepted, and Ruth was betrothed to Boaz. It was final.

Stepping out into the narrow street, the sun blazing above him, Boaz looked at Ruth. He could not help but rejoice at the wide smile on her face and the light that shone in her dark eyes. Was not God perfectly good?

I couldn't believe it. I wanted to jump and shout and twirl in circles for the very delight that filled my heart! Instead, I walked decorously down the narrow street of Bethlehem, turning only once to wave to Boaz, my heart thrilling to see his face lit by the broad smile I had learned to love.

The very deepest desires of my heart had come true. I was to have a loving husband, a home to call my own, and if God willed it, someday I would have children to share in our love. I felt that God had blessed me beyond all imagining, and I could barely contain the thankfulness that filled my heart. As we approached our own gate, Naomi reached over and took my hand, squeezing it gently just for a moment before turning to go into the house.

I, however, turned and walked quickly the short distance to a shady, hidden corner of our field where I often went for the peace of solitude. There, in the silence and privacy of the cool grass, I finally had my time to twirl and laugh and dance. Tears came to my eyes, as once again I was overwhelmed with happiness.

When I began gasping for breath, I dropped in happy exhaustion at the foot of a tree, the thick leaves shading my face as I gazed out over the harvested fields and small homes that made up Bethlehem.

Closing my eyes, I took a deep breath, and instead of trying to pray words to thank God, I simply let my happiness flow through me. I knew that God would know how very thankful I was.

Opening my eyes again I sat up. Shading my face with my hands, I looked as far as I could see down the long, hot road that left the village. I couldn't help but think of my journey on its sandy path, the journey that had brought me here.

I began my physical journey on that road, just I had begun my spiritual journey when I first met Mahlon. I had come so far. At times I doubted, at times I stumbled, but God never let me fail. I can look back now and see him guiding me the whole way. Without him I would not have made it.

Yes, I followed—but it was God's call that captured my heart. Yes, I obeyed—but it was God's love that prompted my obedience. Yes, I was faithful—but it was God's grace that kept me from stumbling. And now it was his goodness that rewarded me.

For God is the great rewarder of those who truly seek him. Remember, my friend, you who have heard my story—remember that God is faithful, and he is good. He rewards his followers. His utter goodness and love will amaze you.

That day, the day of my betrothal to Boaz, I felt God's love more overwhelmingly than ever before. As I turned my steps homeward, I knew that I had reached the end of my journey—a journey begun in faith, carried out in diligence and ended in reward. I had finally entered my place of rest.

This story is taken from Ruth 3 & 4

Reflections

It is Christmastime as I write this. Snow blankets the ground, Christmas carols float through the house, and lights sparkle all around. There is an air of excitement, expectation and warmth that has seeped into every part of our lives, and every person in our home is counting the days until Christmas.

But no one is more excited than my little six-year-old sister Joy. Every day she creeps up the stairs as soon as she awakens, opening another door on her advent calendar, and counting how many more days until she can open her presents.

There is a sweet sincerity and childlike anticipation about Joy that touches my heart. I watch her go about the house every day, now and then coming up to me with wide brown eyes. She can barely hold her excitement in as she talks with me. "Just think Sarah, it's only four more days 'til Christmas!"

As I watched her once again sit on the couch this morning, admiring the lights, and thinking all sorts of exciting little-girl thoughts, I was struck by the realization that I have the same kind of childlike excitement in my own life.

I'm excited because I know that someday I will receive a great reward from God. He is the rewarder of those who seek him. He may require our obedience, faithfulness, and suffering, but none of it escapes his eyes. He is watching, and waiting to reward us when the time is right.

Just like Joy, I can wait in childlike anticipation and excitement, because I know that God is my loving Father, and his reward is better than anything in the world.

I chose to end this book with the story of Ruth because, to me, she is the perfect model of a Christian's life. Like each of us, she had to make a commitment of faith, she had to be diligent, she had to work. But in the end, God brought her a reward that was greater than she could have imagined.

He blessed her with a home, a loving husband, a secure future, and eventually with a sweet little baby named Obed. Her name is remembered for all time, because Obed was the grandfather of David, who was the forefather of Jesus. But ultimately, her greatest reward was to spend eternity with her loving God, in a perfect heaven.

You may still be waiting for your reward. I know I am. In fact, my mom and I were laughing tonight because I couldn't come up with a story of personal reward. But I'm not worried, because I have perfect trust that God has prepared a reward far better than I can even imagine. His love is kinder and more generous than anything in the world.

That is what I want to leave you with. A knowledge of God's overwhelming love for you, and the assurance that a great reward is before you. Your faithfulness, your obedience, your perseverance in times of darkness does matter. God is proud of you, loves you, and is preparing a great reward for all your hard work.

Like Ruth, we will all experience times of diligence, times of faith, but in the end, we will have an overwhelming time of reward. So don't give up, keep on walking ahead, because someday, someday soon, God will bring your reward, and it will be better than you ever imagined.

Read: Hebrews 11:6

Reflect:

How must we come to God? What must we believe? Who does the Lord reward?

Read: John 14:2-3

Reflect:

Where is Jesus' Father's house? What is he preparing for those who follow him? What does he assure his disciples he will do? Someday we will be in the Father's house!

Read: 1 Peter 1:3-4

Reflect:

What has Christ given us because of his mercy? What is kept in heaven for us? Can it ever be taken away from us? What do you think your inheritance in heaven is?

Read: Revelation 22:12

Reflect:

Who is coming soon? What does he bring with him? Do you believe you will be rewarded for your faith? What does the end of the verse describe? This is the person who will reward you!

Journey IV *Ruth*

Journey Journal

_____
_____
_____
_____
_____
_____
_____
_____
_____
_____
_____
_____
_____
_____
_____
_____
_____
_____
_____
_____
_____
_____
_____

Postscript

So, the journeys of these four faithful women come to an end. Each woman walked the road set in front of her with faith and determination, and it is my hope that as you leave the reading of this book, you will be equipped and encouraged to do the same.

I wish I could meet every girl who reads this book, and that we could share stories of our journeys, and encourage one another along the way. For now though, I suppose I'll have to be content with praying for you, even if I don't know your name. But someday I will meet you in heaven, and won't we celebrate then!

In the end, heaven is our final destination, the great reward for which we journey. The knowledge that heaven awaits us is the reason we find the strength to carry on. So in parting, I wish you a heart filled with the joy of the Lord, and a soul that looks forward to heaven. May your journey there be faithful, and marked by stars along the way.

May God bless you as you walk with him.

Postscript